HUMAN RIGHTS ABUSE ON ELDERLY PEOPLE

HUMAN RIGHTS ABUSE ON ELDERLY PEOPLE

Edited by

Dr. S.T. Janetius
Director
Centre for Counselling & Guidance
Sree Saraswathi Thyagaraja College
Pollachi
Tamil Nadu

Dr. V. Kulandaiswamy
Principal
Sree Saraswathi Thyagaraja College
Pollachi
Tamil Nadu
&

Prof. R. Padmanabhan
Dean, Academic Affairs
Sree Saraswathi Thyagaraja College
Pollachi
Tamil Nadu
(India)

DISCOVERY PUBLISHING HOUSE PVT. LTD.
NEW DELHI-110 002

Published by:
Tilak Wasan
DISCOVERY PUBLISHING HOUSE PVT. LTD.
4383/4B, Ansari Road, Darya Ganj
New Delhi-110 002 (India)
Phone : +91-11-23279245, 43596064-65
Fax : +91-11-23253475
E-mail : parul.wasan@gmail.com
discoverypublishinghouse@gmail.com
web : www.discoverypublishinggroup.com

***First Edition:* 2012**

ISBN: 978-93-5056-098-3

Human Rights Abuse on Elderly People

Printed at:
Shree Balaji Art Press
Delhi

Preface

United Nations Organization has estimated that there are 77 million elderly people in India and a third of which are victims of some form of abuse. They are abused in their own homes, at social places and residential cares. In the traditional Indian society joint family system prevailed in which elders enjoyed the benefits of mutual support, concern and help from the members of the family. With the advent of modern sophistication and globalization, the situation in India has taken a dramatic turn. The big families are spilt into small nucleus ones and the bane of discarding the aged crept into current social scenario.

Today the widespread prevalence of unpleasant scene of elderly people being ill-treated and neglected causes dismay and despair to any person with conscience and social concern. There is an increasing downward trend among the family people to look after the elderly which is evidenced by the increasing number of care homes everywhere.

This book is a compilation of various themes and topics presented by scholars in a two days national seminar organized by Sree Saraswathi Thyagaraja College, Pollachi. One of the noteworthy features of the seminar is that it provided a platform for academician as well as social work practitioners and activities to share their empirical experience in diverse regions of the country, which provided a comprehensive picture of the prevailing state of affairs in the contemporary Indian Society.

The objectives for publishing this book would be: to give an exposure to the readers as as well as scholars the prevailing acute problems of elderly people in our society; to create awareness and spread relevant concerns so that new social responsiveness may emerge among the public and policy makers; also educational institutions can plan out some interdisciplinary courses with a view to educate the youth so that value and respect enjoyed by the elders in our society will be restored.

Editors

Contents

PART-II

PART-III

List of Contributors

1. **Dr. Janetius,** Director, Centre for Counselling and Guidance, Sree Sarawathi Thyagaraja College, Pollachi
2. **Dr. John Sundara Raj,** Social Activist and Freelance Writer, Mettupalayam
3. **Dr. C. Swaminathan,** Vice Chancellor Bharathiar University, Coimbatore
4. **Mr. M. Settu,** Director General Sree Saraswathi Thyagaraja College, Pollachi
5. **Mr. P. Govindarajan,** DIG of Prisons, Coimbatore
6. **Dr. K. Nagaraju,** Dept. of Social Work, Sri Ramakrishna Mission Vidyalaya College of Arts and Science, Coimbatore
7. **Ms. Shilpa Thekkechangarampatt,** NSS Student, Thrissur
8. **Ms. Binusha Joie,** Psychology Student, PSGCAS Coimbatore
9. **Dr. Segar,** Dept. of Philosophy, Madras Christian College, Chennai
10. **Prof. C.K. Kotravel Bharathi,** Head, PG Dept. of Management Science, Sree Saraswathi Thyagaraja College, Pollachi
11. **Thanuja Thomas,** Research Scholar, Sri Ramakrishna Mission Vidyalaya College of Arts and Science, Coimbatore
12. **Mrs. R. Ransom Ruth Hephzibah,** Rani Anna Government Arts College for Women. Tirunelveli

    Dr. V. Darling Selvi, Government Arts College for Women, Sivaganga.
13. **Ms. Anbu Selvi,** PG Department of Social Work, Sree Saraswathi Thyagaraja College, Pollachi

14. **R. Renukadevi,** Student, Sree Saraswathi Thyagaraja College, Pollachi
15. **E. Saradha,** Student, Sree Saraswathi Thyagaraja College, Pollachi
16. **Dr. Nawal P. Singh,** SBS College, University of Delhi, Delhi
17. **Mr. B. Sutharsan,** Student, Sree Saraswathi Thyagaraja College, Pollachi
18. **Ms. R. Sandhya,** Student, Sree Saraswathi Thyagaraja College, Pollachi
19. **Mr. Arulappan,** PhD candidate, Puducherry University
20. **Ms. Shoby Bovas,** PG Department of Social Work, Sree Saraswathi Thyagaraja College, Pollachi
21. **Ms. A. Kavitha,** Social Work Trainee, Sree Saraswathi Thyagaraja College, Pollachi
22. **Dr. Mini. T. C.,** HOD, Dept. of Operations Research & Computer Applications, MES College, Idukki
23. **Ms. Meena,** Associate Professor in Commerce, Sree Iyappa College for Women, Nagercoil
24. **Dr. V. Darling Selvi,** Assistant Professor in Commerce, Government Arts College for Women, Sivaganga
25. **Mr. A.P. Senthil Kumar,** CMS College of Science and Commerce, Coimbatore
26. **Mr. Tribhuvan Nath,** Doctoral Candidates, Aligarh Muslim University, Aligarh
27. **Ms. Bushara Bano,** Doctoral Candidate, Aligarh Muslim University, Aligarh
28. **Dr. P. Vyasamoorthy,** Society for Serving Seniors, Secunderabad
29. **Mr. Sailesh Mishra,** Founder President, Silver Inning Foundation and Founder Secretary, ARDSI Greater Mumbai Chapter

PART I

Earthquake in the Empty-nest

A Psycho-social Perspective of Aging

— Dr. Janetius

The urge to grow is one of the insatiable quests of human beings. This process will stop only at the point of death. This growth is different from chronological or biological growth. The personality of a person has different dimensions and will be uncovered at different stages of growth by different means. At one stage in life, a reflecting person will know and feel that half of the life is completed and pause for a while. It is the time to look back and forth to wonder, question and evaluate the dimensions of personal growth and ponder about roads less travelled. Based on this reawakening based on the psychosocial and psychosexual growth, a person will try to redefine the goals and objectives in the light of life experiences, learning and achievements (Levinson, 1978). Psychologists have defined this as midlife transition. This is the stepping stone to maturity. This happens roughly between 45 to 60 years of age. Still further in the growth process, when children leave home after marriage or under job compulsions, elderly people feel that they are left out by everyone and a kind of emptiness surround their lives. This complex phenomenon of emptiness and loneliness in the adult life has been labelled as empty-nest by psychologists

Empty-nest could be a simple feeling of loneliness and emptiness or complex phenomena incorporating many factors. Mental health professionals choose to call it a syndrome because of its complexity in many respects. Since it is a complex experience, adults fail to pinpoint it clearly It could happen at any age or period, but specifically in the adult life or later adult life. When people are confined to home due to retirement it could become a cause of worry and the syndrome shakes the personality like an earthquake. Psychologists have also identified that this feeling is more seen in women than men. It could be due to the fact that men have a lot more opportunities than women to engage themselves in external activities. However, it can happen to both the sexes. A strong parental bond towards the children can aggravate the condition due to role adjustments and changing relationships. Sometimes empty-nest syndrome is compounded by other biological and social life changes happening at that period such as menopause and death of a spouse.

The phenomenon of aging is a multifaceted reality due to the obvious individual differences. Developmental psychology is the field of study dealing with behavioural changes and continuity from conception to old age. Developmental psychology reflects the view that human development throughout the life span is a function of interaction between biologically determined genetic factors and environmental influences, such as family, school, religion, and culture. The virtual importance of heredity and environment in shaping human personality (nature versus nurture; biological genetic factors versus social factors) has long been a topic of debate among psychologists (McCrae, *et al.* 2000). Let us not venture into the complexities of nature *Vs* nurture debate, rather try to understand old age development from an integrative point of view.

As we notice from our day to day living, it is apparent that every human being is different having unique learning experiences, and distinctive genetic characteristics. Yet, there are similarities in many areas that help psychologists define adult development and it is these similarities that cre-ate the hallmarks for well-defined adult development theories and concepts.

Biological and Neuro-endocrine theory of aging high-lights the biological changes and decline seen in the loss of teeth, grey hair or bald head, less muscle strength, poor memory, loss of reproductive ability, accumulation of wrinkles in the skin, chronic joint pains, and the overall physical frailty in the body. The biological aging which is closely associated with the neuro-endocrine theory of aging, states that aging is caused by a progressive loss of sensitivity by the hypothalamus and related structures in the brain and their negative feedback inhibition. This not only disables the process of growth, but also causes post-maturational diseases, aging and death.

Most gerontologists would agree that aging is a set of processes of gradual development and then decline that characterize the life span of an organism. Approximately, above 60 years of age is considered to be late adulthood. It is a complex period of several changes that involve both development and decline. The diversities in the development pattern originate from the concept of life and way of living – like for example, some become less active and some become dynamic; some begin to withdraw and some become more interested in contributing. The developmental processes are also influenced by the outcome reaction to aging and from the thought to compensate for the loss of abilities. The potential conflict arises from the need to compensate behaviours due to the non acceptance of helplessness and the fear of the loss of autonomy. This in fact leads an elderly person even to deviant behaviours.

Menopause refers to that time when spontaneous menstruation ceases for six months to one year. The mean age at which menopause occurs differs from persons to person due to genetic and various environmental conditions; also differ among people of different races, geographical conditions as well as socio-economic situations. Menopause may occur at an earlier age (before 40 years) and is called premature menopause or it can occur very late at age. As women approach menopause, they begin to experience symptoms and signs of *estrogen* deprivation several years in advance by changes in the length of menstrual cycle with various physical and emotional disturbances. The most common symptoms of *estrogen* deprivation include irritability, fatigue, depression, insomnia, loss of memory and headaches. Similar development in men is labelled as *andropause* however it is not defined well as menopause.

Erikson's Psycho-social Development theory perhaps would be one of the best theories which talk about psycho-social development in human beings. The core of Erikson's developmental theory is that 'social environment combined with biological maturation provides an individual with sets of developmental tasks that sometimes causes crises and that need to be faced and resolved in every stage of development so that the next stage of development is smooth and proper'(Erikson, 1968). Psychological, social and emotional development over the life span is sequential during which important inner conflicts are resolved by the interaction of individual self and the living environment. The result of the

Rough Biological Age	Basic Develop-mental Conflict	Significant Life Events	Summary of Development and Consequences
40 to 65 years	Generativity Vs. Stagnation	Parenting	Find some way to satisfy and support the next generation or else feel empty
65 to death	Ego Integrity Vs. Despair	Acceptance of life	Feeling of fulfilment in life or else end your life in despair

resolution of one stage is carried out to the subsequent stage. We will discuss how Erikson defines adulthood and what he talks about the last two stages of human development.

Middle Adulthood typically covers the ages of 40 to 60, and is often viewed as a time of establishing self and thus guiding the next generation; that is, caring for one-self and one's dependents. This is what Erikson (1968) calls 'Generativity', or working to make things better for future generations. This can be achieved by procreativity, productivity or creativity achieved mainly through the commitments made in relationships, and managed with the pursuit of the selected career. In essence, the person becomes involved in caring for something or someone. The person's physical and cognitive functioning remains at their maximum, although physical abilities may begin to decline later in this stage. If this development task is not achieved at this period, stagnation takes place leading to one or other disturbance in the next stage.

Late Adulthood is the period of time from age 60 until death that Erikson (1968) refers to as 'Integrity *vs.* Despair'. The primary focus during this time centres on the understanding the meaning of one's own life, which, if achieved, allows a person to face death without fear. Erikson explains this as achieving a state of *integrity,* which allows a person to reflect back on their life with an appreciation of one's own personal struggles and accomplishments. If one sees his or her life only struggles and no achievement, this period can become highly regretful or bitter about their past and frustrated with their current condition in life. This leads to what Erikson calls despair, which results in fear of death and a potentially miserable existence.

Today since the life expectancy of people have increased dramatically due to major improvements in medicine, nutrition and personal as well as environmental hygiene, this time period has taken a new vigour. Late adulthood becomes a period of 'new opportunities and new relationships' where a person can develop new skills and potentials (Kegan, 1982). While physical abilities often diminish, psychological and social growth often increase here, as most of the people during this stage could still seek for new personal meaning through professional commitments.

General characteristics: Late adulthood cannot be defined by the chronological age because better living conditions and the enhanced health care facilities that are available today extend the middle adulthood to a lengthy period and people don't enter into latter adulthood sometimes until 65+ years. The latter adulthood often referred as old age could be divided into two parts: early old age (roughly up to 70), and advanced old age (above 70).

We will look at both these periods together as one period. The main characteristics of this period would be: (*a*) a time of physical and mental decline, (*b*) a period of blessing for some people in the sense they consider it as a period of rest from active life where as for some it may be a period of curse and boredom; this individual difference is very significant, (*c*) social negative attitude is very explicit leading to self-definition and self-pitying as old and invalid person leading further to pessimistic self concept, (*d*) role changes from the active social and professional life to passive life and, (*e*) poor adjustments to various life situations. All the above mentioned issues lead the elderly person primarily to adjustment issues with the self, in the families and also society.

Cultural Adjustment in the old age is the most neglected aspect of adult development. It is a major adjustment need due to the nature of changing society. Modern Indian society and the creeping globalised culture have forced elders to feel the pinches of empty-nest syndrome more than any time in the past. The younger generation finds it hard to manage the traditional values imposed by the elders and the elders fail to realise the changing cultural values thus creating a big generation gap.

As the extended families are becoming less common these days, the elderly people are not prepared mentally to live alone at homes or feel comfortable in the aged-homes. Unlike the Western countries where elders are accustomed to be alone in the old age, cultures such as Africa and Asia where traditionally elderly parents are held in very high esteem and the duty to care for them and respect them remains strongly in the psyche of the people. Let me give you two current examples from our country to state that this traditional concept has not disappeared or the need to eradicate the same is not acceptable to many. The recent Rajasthan government ruling that it is a criminal offense to neglect the parents and the children are liable. Another example would be the recent survey conducted by Canara, HSBC, Oriental Bank of Commerce.

Life Insurance (2009) which states that India has the higher saving ratio compared to other countries but 35% saving go for their children and 12% for their retirement. Indians save for their children thinking that they will take care of them when they are old, rather than securing their own retirement period. Although this is the trend reflected in the recent survey, the more the cities become westernized and industrialized, the threat to the traditional values are evident and the elders become vulnerable.

Vocational Adjustment is also one of the areas in which Indians are not prepared at all. On the eve of retirement I asked an employee what he is planning to do after retirement and he gleefully answered, "to say the fact, I haven't thought about it Sir". This explains the pathetic situation in our country. Adjustment to retirement and life after retirement is an area that needs a lot of focus today. People need to prepare themselves for retirement so that they are properly oriented for their old age phase in life. A well prepared retired life could be presumably a period of happiness. Pre-retirement counselling will be of great help for people to face the challenges of new phase in their life and well prepared for the retirement life.

Another factor that determines the happiness or sorrow regarding retirement or vocational adjustment in old age is whether retirement is voluntary or compulsory. Desire to work, desire to rest and economical situation are the factors that play key roles here. If a person takes retirement voluntary, he is better adjusted. If not s/he will be in identity crisis, looking for substitute activities. This search itself will become a pain. Economic status makes a world of difference in the retirement adjustment. Besides these, good marriage, attitude of family members to help them and well planned hobbies and occupation give better adjustment in the post retirement stage.

Family Adjustment mainly with the spouse is of top priority because the elderly people spend a lot of time in the house. Spouses with similar interests adjust better, interact better. Changes in sexual behaviour are also a concern in family adjustment. Sexual problems and issues could be identified from four concepts: People believe that there is no sex life in old age due to physical changes; antagonistic relationships leads to less taste for sex life; incompatibility with spouse also contribute to the lesser appetite and problematic sexual adjustment; social attitude towards sexuality inhibits elderly people to abstain from sex life. Psychologists have identified that decline in sexual desire is more of psychological than physiological problem.

Other family adjustment issues are: relationship with children and grandchildren, adjustment to the loss of spouse and or remarriage. Remarriage can be a good supportive alternative for people who lose their partners in the old age. In a traditional community like ours, where marriage is often associated with sex and procreation, people look negatively at old people when they remarry. However, remarriage is one of the best alternatives and coping mechanism for a loner, as it paves way for companionship in the old age. Care should be taken in identifying partners of similar education, social background because in the old age people don't learn to adjust to ordinary issues. Approval from children to marry too contributes to the happiness in latter adult marriage.

Elders as Victims as Well as Persecutors: Lack of adjustment to the above mentioned areas place the elders in a precarious situation of both victims as well as persecutors.

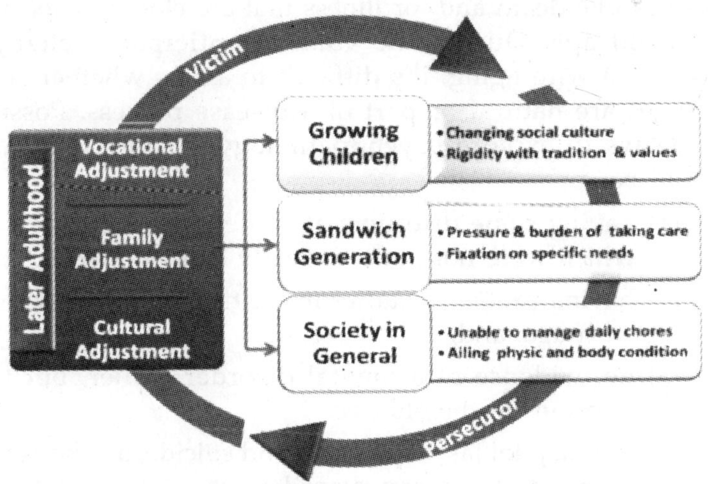

Elders in a vicious cycle as well as persecutors

In the eyes of the growing children, the non-ability of the elders to understand and adopt the changing cultural values and the modern social trends, on top of all, rigidity in holding personal likes and dislikes make them persecutors. These again lead to victimization from the part of younger generation. For the sandwich-generation, elders are an added burden in their daily struggle with their children. The fixations of elders for specific needs and demands add fuel to this issue. In the modern urban as well as semi-urban settings, where both the couple go for job, it is rather inconvenient and impractical to attend the needs of one's own parents in every detail. Added to that, is the bitter fact that some elders are abusive and repressive. Take for example our familiar mother-in-law stories. Here too, they are forcefully placed in a vicious cycle of being both the persecutors and the victims.

In addition, the weak physical body and the inability to do many chores place the elders in various social situations in the same vicious cycle.

Psychopathology in Old Age is a very complex phenomenon to be studied mainly due to the inevitable realities like death and/or illness that are closely associated with old age. Due to the various anticipated changes associated with aging, it's difficult to assess whether some changes are natural or part of a disease process. Possible pathways to explore psychopathology in later adulthood would be:

(1) having some disorders at earlier points in one's life which were not noticed clearly or identified;

(2) having problems earlier in life that gets more serious with age; and,

(3) no evidence of a mental disorder earlier, but that develops in the old age.

Dementia, phobias, depression and suicide, alcoholism or alcohol dependence, sleep disorders are the major health hazards related to old age. Other health problems that are chronic and common in late adulthood are: arthritis, osteoporosis and hypertension. Besides these, heart disease, cancer, and cerebrovascular diseases are also prevalent. With regular exercise, proper nutrition with diet and weight control better health can be achieved. Antioxidants can counteract the cell damage. Monitored intake of antioxidants (vitamin C, vitamin E, and beta-carotene) in the form of food or medicinal intake can slow the aging process. Protections from environmental pollutions and other hazards and non-exposure to the risk of being sick can increase well being among the elderly.

Psycho-social Management Strategies for a Better Old Age: Certain strategies are expected of elders in order to manage the old age. In the first place, one should have been blessed with a better lived and fulfilled first part of the life that would reduce despair and frustrations of life at the old age period. Secondly one of the most neglected aspects in the Indian scenario is the lack of preparation for retirement life. A well prepared retirement life, in terms of economic security, relevant social networking, needed vocational/professional pursuits and good free time activities and hobbies, can reduce the turmoil of old age to a greater extent. Thirdly developing a broader mindset to accept and manage the changing cultural values is a must from the part of elders because the globalization and change of cultural values are unavoidable realities today. Earthquakes can shake the old age but can't destroy the happiness if old age is well planned and adequately prepared.

REFERENCES

Erikson, E.H. (1968). *Identity: Youth and Crisis.* New York: Norton

Kegan, R. (1982). *The evolving self: problem and process in human development. Cambridge*, MA: Harvard University Press.

Levinson, D. (1978). *Seasons of a man's life*. New York: Knopf.

McCrae, Robert R.; Costa, Paul T., Jr.; Ostendorf, Fritz; Angleitner, Alois; Høebíèková, Martina; Avia, Maria D.; Sanz, Jesús; Sánchez-Bernardos, Maria L.; Kusdil, M. Ersin; Woodfield, Ruth; Saunders, Peter R.; Smith, Peter B. (2000). Nature over nurture: Temperament, personality, and life span development. *Journal of Personality and Social Psychology*, Vol 78(1), 173-186.

Last Steps of Life the Most Painful

(The Origin and Evolution of Natural-Law and Human Rights)

— Dr. John Sundara Raj

Introduction

The problem of the elderly people is becoming one of the major problems of the society. It is also part and parcel of the modern society, which is industrialized and advanced. It is something new to the modern society of India. India is traditionally known for living in groups and hamlets and major civilizations which sprout from India or Asia. The famous Indus Valley civilization in which people settled near the banks of river Indus wherein the people lived in groups and in patriarchal family atmosphere. So there is a mutual support and concern and help for each other and lived under the guidance of the elders in the family. The value system was different. The elder is respected and the earnings are shared. The modernization and the influence of the west came in; the situation in India also changed. The big collective families segregated into small nucleus family. This is one of the major reasons for the discard of the aged. There was no place for the elder and the aged.

Abuse at home and family: Knowingly or unknowingly there is discomfort in the family for the elderly persons. Both partners of the nucleus family are supposed to go for job to sustain the family. The family set up is becoming more and more private and sensitive. There is no tolerance in the family in both sides.

Abuse in the Society: Incidents of aged people being deserted on the streets are on the rise. Neither the children care for their parents nor society has a system to support them. It is pathetic that even the administrative systems do not have an organized procedure to assure decent last days for the senior citizens. Offering concessions to senior citizens would be just populist schemes but there has to be a system to prevent senior citizens becoming orphans.

Increasing number of such old people is warning signal for those earning today to save for the future so that they could fend for themselves when they could not earn their livelihood.

Abuse in the Workplaces: Being particularly vulnerable, the elderly are "often ignored and denied their full human rights," according to the Council of Europe's Commissioner for Human Rights Thomas Hammarberg, as revealed in his writing on the council's website on 28 April 2008. The author calls for the human dignity of the "lost generation" to be respected and their rights restored, as they do not enjoy an adequate standard of living and many of them are poor. Given their frailty, aged people should get "special protection", Hammarberg argues, explaining that this is why the Universal Declaration of Human Rights stipulated they have the right to security.

In our society, the elderly tend to be discriminated against on several levels and may be considered as worthless or non-productive, as stated by the human rights commissioner states. Hammarberg highlights the labour market as a good example of an area where discrimination frequently occurs – many retired people who wish to continue their professional activity do not have the opportunity to do so as their age prevents them from accessing the market. The author suggests leaders should make retirement ages more flexible as "older persons should have the opportunity to work as long as they wish and are able to satisfy the norms of performance and productive work".

Modern society in the opinion of Hammerberg, has not adequately addressed disabilities caused by ageing like reduced vision, reduced hearing or reduced mobility, which reinforces the necessity of designing policies and programmes that would adapt to their situation.

Institutionally, he says some countries should exercise better control over the way in which aged people are treated, as they are "less able to defend themselves against abuse". He also calls for the conditions in which they are hosted to be more thoroughly monitored. Faced with ageing populations, the elderly are bound to be "a strain on the social and health care system," therefore the commissioner urges European leaders to re-examine their social protection systems, health care and housing policies, which are not "suited" to the elderly.

Highlighting the Problem

- The transition from joint family to nuclear family is the primary problem
- The globalization and industrialization is another reason
- The influence of western culture on our traditional culture
- The move of the value system from one to another
- The intolerance among people
- The misunderstanding of the young and the aged
- The sense of privacy among the young people
- Non existence of adequate laws to control the problem
- The perception of affective of human life is vanishing and the mechanic life is replaced with

- Now it is all Money centred materialism rather than value centred
- Respect for the elder is lost and love for the younger is decreasing

Law and the Areas of Violation: The concept of human rights – United Nations Universal Declarations of Human Rights: When we talk about human rights we assume that there are some fundamental and universal principles which govern or ought to govern all genuine human relations. Over the centuries in human history, these principles are supposed to have evolved in the conscience of peoples and nations and acquired higher degrees of clarity and universality.

One of the most recognized statements of these principles is the United Nations Universal Declaration of Human Rights in 1948. Article 1 of this Declaration says:

> "All human beings are born free and equal in dignity and rights. They are endowed with reason and conscience and should act towards one another in the spirit of brotherhood."

The United Nations General Assembly proclaimed the Universal Declaration of Human Rights "as a common standard of achievement for all peoples and all nations" and called upon all "to secure their universal and effective recognition of observance." When the Universal Declaration of Human Rights was proclaimed by the General Assembly, it was viewed as the first step in the formulation of an "International Bill of Rights" that would have legal as well as moral force among the international communities.

In 1976, "three decades after this comprehensive undertaking was launched by the United Nations", the "International Bill of Human Rights" became a reality, with the entry into force of three significant instruments:

1. The International Covenant on Economic, Social and Cultural Rights
2. The International Covenant on Civil and Political Rights
3. The optional Protocol to the latter covenant.

Evolution of 'Human Rights': The concept of Human Rights and its recognition and observance among the peoples and nations of the world have been growing both in content and in the universality of its application. Three important stages can be distinguished within this process:

1. Primordial simple societies in which members were part of a community
2. Encounters with outsiders and the emergence of complex societies
3. Modern political societies in which individuals are citizens with equality before the law. Primordial simple societies were homogeneous self-contained communities.

Life in these communities was cantered around certain values which all the members shared. These values were held together by a central authority of the chieftain, ruler or king.

All members enjoyed certain equality and had rights and duties which were based on the common value system. The individuals were part of a whole. Outsiders were strangers, or enemies. They had no rights. The principle of rights and duties did not apply to them. Homogenous, self-contained communities could not survive very long. As they encountered new group with different values and power base, there was intense conflict. In the process some were exterminated, others subjugated or reduced to various degrees of inequality. They were forced to live in the midst of other groups and political systems and were subjected to various degrees of tolerance or rejection by the dominant groups. There was no perception or recognition at this stage of human equality and human rights going beyond one's own group.

Gradually, a new form of society was formed with political boundaries and a central authority. Rupert Emerson calls it "the terminal community", the largest community which "effectively" commands men's loyalty" overriding the claims of all others. Al other identities religious, cultural, ideological —have to exist within it and subservient to it.

Citizenship and Human Rights: In the modern political society social relations underwent further changes. The members of the new society became citizens with rights and duties. A central value system was projected which claimed to be the value system of all the people of that society. A political centre was also formed which claimed to represent all the citizens.

The reality however was very different. The political institution was controlled by the dominant groups of that society. The central value system also was the value system of the dominant groups. The new society was in fact a conglomeration of diverse social groups with unequal power base and social status and controlled by the dominant groups. The weaker groups were marginalised, exploited and were relegated to lower social status. Equality before law and equal opportunities were not available to them. They carried on a double existence: the identity of their primordial communities which lost its legal recognition and was reduced to the "private" realm, and the citizenship in the new political society, the benefits of which were far from their reach.

Although controlled and manipulated by the dominant groups, new political societies unwittingly gave rise to two important consequences. First, it implied, at least in principle, the recognition of citizenship for all individuals within a particular political society including those who belonged to various marginalized groups. Second, the idea of citizenship also implied the recognition of equality before the law. It did not matter that the recognition of these principles did not automatically lead to actual practice. It would take a long time before their observance became a reality. And the observance itself would depend not on the recognition of the principles but on the actually existing power relations within society. Whether you are treated equally or whether your rights are violated will depend on how much power or influence you wield in the political arena. The less your influence is the less your voice will be heard. Equality is not given, equality is to be taken. Yet a process was set in motion. More and more marginalized groups would soon begin to claim equality of membership in the new society and their rights flowing from this membership. They would also begin to re-assert their identity, dignity and equality before the law, equal opportunities and a share in the nation-building process.

The process of defining the principles of human rights and their extension to new areas and groups continued and today embraces the international communities of the whole world. The United Nations Universal Declaration of Human Rights is the latest and the most comprehensive expression of this process.

We have still a long way to go. The concept of "Human Rights", as it has developed, is based on the concept of the individual abstracted from his concrete living context. The assumption seems to be that individuals belonging to the state constitute a homogeneous community. All differences, identities and value systems within the state are either ignored or rejected and are replaced by a central law and value system created and interpreted by the dominant groups.

This process will have to be reversed. The individual belongs to a community with an identity and value system. The communities exist in complex pluralistic societies. The modem political societies are part of an international community. Relationships, rights and duties exist at all these levels. The concept of human rights, therefore, must include all these units and interaction between them in order to develop equitable relations.

An important factor that affects the interaction between different units is the presence of national and international institutions - social, economic and political. It is important to examine how these various institutions and regional groupings affect the various human groups at different levels, positively and negatively.

The formulation and application of human rights has also been culturally bound. The western socio-cultural experience dominated this process; focus on the individual, the stress on right to property, the concept of sovereignty of the political societies are the examples of this.

Human Right Violations in India

Collectives and Culture Rights are basic for all human beings. While the political system of the country offers citizens individual rights, the state negates Collective Rights to socio-religious groups. The Indian state system is a colonial construction and is ill-equipped to provide rights and justice on the basis of culture of communities. In the liberal discourse on rights because of the homogenization of the language and practice of rights very scant attention is paid to the rights of the collectives based on their culture. In the western perspective given its industrial economy, conditions are created for the development of individuals. The language of rights is closely associated with the capitalist form of economy. Materialism is connected to an individual way of life. There is a lack of regard for social obligations, material dependence and the solidarity of the social whole. In the Indian understanding at least for several groups in the country rights are more centred on communities than individuals. The existence and development of individuals is in the context of the community, given the inherited network of social attachments. Family, community and neighbourhood determine one's life and existence for several groups in India and individuals are located.

Rights of the Collectives—Indian Context

It is important and urgent therefore to locate cultural communities within the political community of the nation and provide them autonomy for their development within the community.

The Indian socio-economic and political formation is of dominant caste character. While exalting dominant values such system dismisses indigenous and minority values and cultures as insignificant and inferior. As a result the rights of Collectives are violated even today in the name of rule of law and democracy. The caste system deprived indigenous groups of their rights in the name of God. The Collectives are deprived of their rights by the very same state system meant to protect them in the name of order, protection, welfare and development. Thus both society and state through hegemonic violence have attempted to destroy the life and existence of these indigenous and minority groups even to the extent of depriving these groups their right to life. The threat to the existence and life style of these groups is more acute today than ever before. **"Hindutva",** a theology of the ruling classes through which caste forces are further strengthened is posing a threat to the life of the Collectives. Recent events in Nagaland, Mizoram, Arunachal Pradesh, Jharkhand and Chhattisgarh are places where tribal communities should be made sovereign over all matters pertaining to their life and existence.

Public Government: It is a government organized over geographically defined territory where residents include both Collectives and Non-Collectives. Since the Collectives are a majority, they retain power permitting the non-Collectives their rights to life and existence. The Dalits, tribals and even minorities can come under the type of government in some areas of the country.

Community of Interest Government: A government of the type is based on such matters as common interests in cultural and other matters like housing, education, health, religion and economic development. Membership would be based on the specific identity of the group and voluntary affiliation. Given the fact that the Collectives are distributed over an area, the jurisdiction and authority of course would be limited. The constitution has already granted certain minority rights for religious Collectives in India which are detested by the majority. What is important at present is to further expand them to include certain other areas and provide sovereign power in specific areas so that the Collectives are well protected.

Because the life of the Collectives is different and characterized by values of community, self-government is fundamental to preserve and protect the rights of the Collectives in India. Patterned on the liberal constitutions of the West, the Indian Constitution has argued for individual rights. Recognizing rights of Collectives even at this point will ensure the cultural integrity of Collectives. One may even argue that small scale societies or communities are too factionalised to enable fair governance and leadership. However self-government is the inherent right of the Collectives. What should be demanded at this point is that the central government should be invited to alter the Constitution to provide rights for Collectives. The governments for the Collectives can be federal, provincial or self-rule. Each of these governments should be sovereign within their own spheres as far as the rights of the Collectives are entry into force of three significant instruments:

1. The International Covenant on Economic, Social and Cultural Rights;
2. The International Covenant on Civil and Political Rights; and
3. The optional Protocol to the latter covenant.

Conclusion

Evolution of "Human Rights": The concept of Human Rights and its recognition observance among the peoples and nations of the world have been growing both in content and in the universality of its application. Three important stages can be distinguished within this process:

1. Primodial simple societies in which members were part of a community;
2. Encounters with outsiders and the emergence of complex societies; and
3. Modem political societies in which individuals are citizens with equality before the law.

Primordial simple societies were homogeneous self-contained communities. Life in these communities was centred on certain values which all the members shared. These values were held together by a central authority of the chieftain, ruler or king. All members enjoyed certain equality and had rights and duties which were based on the common value system. The individuals were part of a whole. Outsiders were strangers, or enemies. They had no rights. The principle of rights and duties did not apply to them. Homogeneous, self-contained communities could not survive very long. As they encountered new groups with different values and power base, there was intense conflict. In the process some were exterminated, others subjugated or reduced to various degrees of inequality. They were forced to live in the midst of other groups and political systems and were subjected to various degrees of tolerance or rejection by the dominant groups. There was no perception or recognition at this stage of human equality and human rights going beyond one's own group. Gradually, a new form of society was formed with political boundaries and a central authority. Rupert Emerson calls it '"the terminal community", the largest community which "effectively commands men's loyalty" overriding the claims of all others. All other identities—religious, cultural, ideological—have to exist within it and subservient to it.

Human Rights Abuse on Elderly People —*An Overview*

— Dr. C. Swaminathan

Human Right Act, 1993 says that "Human Rights mean the rights relating to life, liberty, equality and dignity of the individual guaranteed by the Constitution or embodied in the International Covenants and enforceable by courts in India." The concept of Human Right is a 20th century concept. It was traditionally known as natural rights or the rights of man. In the 18th century in Europe, several political philosophers developed the concept of 'natural right' in line with the law of nature. These are the rights belonging to a person by nature and because he is a human being and not by virtue of his citizenship in a particular country or membership in a particular religion or ethnic group.

A Human Right Regime came in India with the inauguration of the Constitution in 1950. Human Rights concept in traditional India is different from the modern understanding. There, the society acted as a guarantor, but today it is the state that maintains rights. Hence, in spite of emerging human rights consciousness, everywhere, there are violations. Violations are not from the state apparatus alone, violations took place at family, neighbourhood, work place, and by various non-state actors like religion, political parties and other ethnic and cultural groups.

First of all it is necessary to understand what elder abuse is. Various authors have defined elder abuse but a comprehensive definition is given by Council of Europe (1992). They define elder abuse as:

> "A non-accidental act of omission, which undermines the life, the physical and psychological integrity of an older person or harms the development of his her personality and or undermines or damages his or her financial security."

Abuse has been broadly classified into six categories:

(1) **Physical abuse:** This includes beating, pushing, slapping, and sexual abuse

(2) **Psychological abuse:** This includes verbal threatening to abuse the older person, isolation, moral blackmail, threat or admitting them to in old age homes, insulting, ignoring, and withholding affection etc.

(3) **Financial abuse:** Which is misappropriation or properly through fair or foul means

(4) **Denial of rights:** like keeping in isolation, preventing one from practicing one's religion, denying the right to vote

(5) **Active neglect:** In the form of refusal or failure to undertake care taking obligations

(6) **Passive neglect:** This is refusal or failure to fulfil a care taking obligation

In real life, in most of the cases, there is a combination of all these types of abuses.

United Nations Organization has estimated that 77 million elderly people are in India and one third of elderly victims are abused in their own homes. Surveys reveal that almost 30% of India's elderly persons are subject to some form of abuse or neglect by their families. Paradoxically, in spite of this, only one in six of the abused elderly reports the injustice. Shockingly, 47.3% of abuse against elders is committed by adult caregivers, partners of family members, while 48.7% of all abuse cases imply neglect of an elderly person, abandonment, physical, financial or emotional abuse.

In the traditional Indian families, there was a mutual support, concern and help for elders in the family. The modernization and the influence of the West came in, the situation has changed. The big collective families are segregated into small nucleus families and the discard of the aged started to creep into the social scenario.

Today the widespread scene is one of dismay and neglect. There is nobody to look after the elderly people. An increasing number of the elderly are now looking for employment, mostly for low wages, and under insecure and unhealthy working conditions. As the society is moving from traditional to modern, from joint families to nuclear families, the increasing incidents of abuses are becoming common phenomena. This changing global phenomenon is that the traditional Indian social and family bonds are not as strong as seen in the past and elders are being marginalized.

In the developed countries, elderly people have the governmental support systems in the form of social security in which free or discounted medical care as well as institutionalized home care are provided. In the Indian subcontinent no such significant social security system to take care of the elderly are commonly available. Although the government has integrated many medical policies and pension schemes for the benefit of retiring government employees, the people who work in the private sector as well as marginal labourers are often the victims of abuse due to economical constraints.

Every year World Elder Abuse Awareness Day is being observed on June 15th. It serves as a call-to-action for individuals, organizations, and communities to raise awareness about elder abuse, neglect, and exploitation. World Elder Abuse Awareness Day is an opportunity to share information about abuse, neglect, and exploitation in later life. However, raising awareness of mistreatment of elder persons is an ongoing effort, not limited to one day.

In the emerging scenario, universities and colleges have to play an important role. National Policy on Education has also emphasized the need for human right education through the promotion of values such as of heritage, democracy, secularism, access, equity, protection and removal of social barriers etc. For this, development of courses on human rights has to be a continuous exercise to be developed through workshops, for better collective thinking and social actions. The courses must reflect the national concern and regional emphasis.

Further, mere knowledge about human rights is not sufficient unless there is an understanding as to how human rights can easily become vulnerable to abuse by various structures and processes of power. With the aims of sensitizing and changing the attitude mind and creating a human right culture, the role of teaching methods remain crucial in the achievement of objectives. With the present state of teaching methodology, imparting education of concern would make the human rights education more academic. It is important to have practical oriented teaching – bringing in field experiences in the classrooms and taking students to community.

All we will be elders one day and join the ever increasing percentage of senior citizens in the global population. And yet some of us continue to show gross indifferences and disrespect to our elders in our own families and in the society. Each of us might have countless reasons, logics and excuses for this behaviour but this could be due to combination of many problems. Let us try to put into a right perspective these various problems and what we could do to keep our elders happy. By helping our elders stay physically fit and mentally happy, we are only helping ourselves and our future. It we fail to give proper care and respect to our elders now at home we will get the same ugly treatment from our children later on in our lives!

Elderly People and Abuses in the Indian Context

— Mr. M. Settu

When we are talking about our Indian economy and its future, we always quote and say with pride that half of our population is under the age of 25. The youngest nation in the world and we call this as the Demographic Dividend or Population Dividend. This is only the greener side of the coin. But if we look at the other side of the age-group, it is a worrying fact.

With improving health care, our average life expectancy has gone up from 57 years in 1990 to 65 years today. In the next 20 years, India will be the home to the world's second-largest population of the elderly people. This age-wave means that the number of senior citizens is expected to touch 200 million in 2030.

The total world population of the elderly people was five percentage in 1980; it has risen sharply in the last three decades. The percentage of elderly people would be around 15 percentage in 2030. Out of which 70 percentage would live in the developing countries like India. And one out of every seven elders in the world would be living in India. And in that elderly population, 40 percentage are below poverty line and 70 percentage are illiterates.

India has always been proud of its enduring family values. The symbol of these values was the large joint family system, with three generations living under one roof. The value for elders is better explained in one of the chapters of our Manusmriti as follows:

"One who always serves and respects elderly is blessed with four things: Long Life, Wisdom, Fame and Power"

–Manusmriti Chapter 2:121.

Also in a Chinese proverb -

"Those young who show no respect to their elders achieve nothing worth mentioning when they grow up." –Confucius.

The great Tamil poet Thiruvalluvar points out this way:

The way if showing filial devotion is to make others exclaim within the hearing of the father, what penance the father must have performed to beget such a son.

With rapid urbanization, the Indian joint family system got fragmented and nuclear family units became the order of the day. We were all thinking and believing that this change would never affect the basic assumption of looking after the parents and elders. But that is no more the fact. With today's changing lifestyles, modern technology and growing prosperity, our working population must answer the very difficult question: ***How do we look after those who looked after us?***

This is a greatest challenge for both the children and the elders. India's senior citizens feel vulnerable, lonely or abandoned. They may have lost a spouse or their children would have gone abroad or in cases of abuse, they have been sent out of homes.

The children are now sandwiched between looking after their own family and caring for old parents. Some of them have money to take care of their parents but they may not have enough time for giving proper attention.

Old age is the end of the human life cycle. Besides an increased level of illness, the aging process leads to many disabilities such as low vision and blindness resulting from cataracts, deafness resulting from nerve impairment, loss of mobility from arthritis and a general inability to care for oneself.

Definition of Elder Abuse: Elder abuse is the mistreatment of elders; it is a phenomenon of inter-personal violence. The UK's *Action on Elder Abuse* developed a definition subsequently adopted by the International Network for the Prevention of Elder Abuse.

It states Elder Abuse as follows:

> *"Elder abuse is a single or repeated act or lack of appropriate action, occurring within any relationship where there is an expectation of trust which causes harm or distress to an older person."*

In general, ***Elder abuse*** has been categorized under five headings as follows:

1. ***Physical abuse***: Causing physical pain or injury or wound by striking, physical coercion, imposing punishment causing physical agony, slap marks; kick marks, burns such as cigarette burns, malnutrition.
2. ***Psychological/emotional abuse***: Humiliation, ridiculing, threatening with shouting, causing fear and anxiety, denial of basic rights like choice or giving opinion or privacy.
3. ***Financial/material abuse***: The illegal or improper exploitation and/or use of funds or resources; stealing bank passbook or pension book; forced to give power of attorney and using their money for their selfish purpose; forced transfer of money or assets.
4. ***Sexual abuse***: Unacceptable contact of any kind with an older person; forcing them to watch unnecessary videos; unwelcome talk about sex etc.
5. ***Neglect***: Lack of basic care, failure to provide proper health care, proper food and proper cloth; abandon-

ment; being left to sit in urine/faeces; not providing mobility aids and hearing aids; isolation by locking in a room; not allowing them to have any social contact;

With this background of understanding, let us ask some questions like:

- How to avoid or reduce this elder abuse?
- What methods are available to the senior citizens to take care of themselves?
- What are the various human rights available to them to protect from this abuse?
- What are the constitutional supports available to them?
- What are government policies and legal framework applicable to them to go for remedial actions?
- And, finally how do we bring about a great awareness on this subject both to the elders, the caretakers and the youth, in general?

Conclusion

In conclusion let me recall some great literature to stimulate your minds.

> *There may be salvation for those who have killed all other virtues, but not for the one who has killed gratitude. I would say this is most applicable to those who are not grateful to their parents and elders.* —Thiruvalluvar (110)

> *"The real test of any civilization of a nation would be understood from the way by which the nation treats their elders"*

Let us bring back an awareness on our culture and value system to respect and shower true love on our elders.

Human Rights Abuses on Elders

With Special Reference to Prisons

— Mr. P. Govindarajan

The life expectancy having increased from 40 years in 1951 to 65 years today, a person toady has 25 years more to live than he would have 50 years back. Because of the prolonged life expectancy, the elderly population has many problems. Unlike in traditional Indian society, the elders are being abused even in their fundamental rights. Now India is having 77 million elderly population, and this population is also growing to grow 177 million in next 25 years. In this aging scenario, there is a tremendous pressure to look after the elderly population. Due to the present cyber culture and globalization the traditional Indian joint families are split into small nucleus families. Due to this type of family disorganization, the aged parents are forced to stay in the Aged Homes. These types of homes are growing rapidly in India and Globalization and modernization have added fuel to the issue.

Causes of Challenges: Large volume of authentic data on demographic trends, impact of changes in the family structure and migration, physical and behavioural status, organization and dynamics of health stems exist in Indian literature.

However, very little effort has been made to develop a model of health and social care in tune with the changing need and time. As no model for older people exists in India, as well as most other societies with similar socio-economic situation, it may be a challenge as well as opportunity for innovation in healthy system development. This is a major challenge because: (*i*) no clear policy or strategy for development of health care of older people exists, (*ii*) there are differences in opinion whether there is a need for such segregation; (*iii*) there is dilemma about the most effective way of satisfying the health needs of the elderly and (*iv*) there is no unanimity regarding minimum knowledge and skills required in the curriculum of health professionals.

Need for Study: It is often simplistically considered that health problems in old age are a constellation of problems such as increased susceptibility to infection, inability to cope with physical and psychological stress, degenerative arthritis, atherosclerotic and vascular diseases of heart and brain, cancer of various organs and cognitive impairments due to declining brain size or more importantly various types of cognitive disorders. However, data from focused academic research as well as three nation wide sample surveys of 1986-1987, 1995-1996 and 2004 reveal that the magnitude and nature of diseases and disabilities of old age may be much more that what has been summarized in the previous statement. How the society has to face the challenge? A strategy is the need of the hour. The components of old age care strategy could be iterative process of policy and strategy formulation, focus on primary health care , age friendly health systems, strong participation of the older population in society, development of human resources for quality health care, creation and maintenance of multidisciplinary networks to facilitate care of the elderly, research, surveys and studies for establishment of a database for evidence based care and raising the awareness of the population to active ageing. Health in old age is affected by social and Economic system? For a society like ours, probably a balanced mix of both these models should be more pertinent and of great value. Long-term care is the system of activities undertaken by informal caregivers (family, friends, and/ or neighbours) and/or professionals (health, social & others) to ensure that a person who is not fully capable of self-care can maintain the highest possible quality of life, according to his or her individual preferences, with the greatest possible degree of Independence, autonomy, participation, personal fulfilment and human dignity. Long-term care for older person in India has always been a matter of family functioning.

Currently, no old age home or senior citizen accommodation provides shelter to older people with mental and physical disability requiring assistance in activities of daily living and intense nursing care. Irrespective of economic status the care givers of such individuals undergo great stress in caring such disabled relatives and also lead their own lives. Older people living alone without any surviving caregivers also need long term care at some point of time or the other.

Human Rights of Elderly People: Let us discuss human rights that appear most relevant to particular difficulties potentially faced by older people, i.e. persons aged 65 years and older.

Section 1 highlights key areas in which older people may face particular difficulties.

Section 2 explains that older people have human rights under the Human Rights Act 1998 that potentially protect their interests when facing difficulties in these areas.

Section 3 complies a list of human rights that appear most relevant to older people, and provides examples illustrating when they could be applied. Section 4 highlights key principles that govern the scope of these rights.

Key Areas in which Older People may Face Particular Difficulties

Older people may face particular difficulties in the following key areas:

- Physical and mental health
- Community care
- Transport
- Employment; income
- Education and leisure
- Utilities and consumer protection
- Access to information
- Decision-making

Human Rights in Prison

Crime is the outcome of a diseased mind and jail must
Have and environment of hospital for treatment and care.

—Mahatma Gandhi

Never before in its history, prison administration in India was subjected to such a critical review by the higher judiciary as in the last few decades. Discarding its erstwhile "hands off" doctrine towards prisons, the Supreme Court of India came strongly in favour of judicial scrutiny and intervention whenever the rights of prisoners in detention or custody were found to have been infringed upon. In *Sunil Batra* V. *Delhi Administration and Other* (1978), Mr. Justice V.R. Krishna Iyer pronounced: "prisoner have enforceable liberties, devalued may be but not demonetized; and under our basic scheme, Prison Power must bow before Judge Power, if fundamental freedoms are in jeopardy". Again in *Sunil Batra* V. *Delhi Administration* (1979, the Court asked and affirmed: "Are prisoner" persons? Yes, of course. To answer in the negative is to convict the nation and the Constitution of dehumanization and to repudiate the world legal order, which now recognises rights of prisoners in the International Covenant on Prisoners' Rights to which our country has signed assent".

In a number of judgments on various aspects of prison administration, the Supreme Court of India has laid down three broad principles:

(*i*) a person in prison does not become a non-person.

(*ii*) A person in prison is entitled to all human rights within the limitations of imprisonment.

(*iii*) There is no justification in aggravating the suffering already inherent in the process of incarceration.

Obviously, these principles have serious implications for prison administration. They not only call for a thorough restructuring of the prison system in terms of the humanisation of prison conditions, minimum standards for institutional care, reorientation of prison of prison staff, reorganization of prison programmes and rationalization of prisons rules and regulations. From this viewpoint, among the various directives by the Supreme Court of India, in *Sunil Batra* V. *Delhi Administration* (1979), the following deserve a special mention:

"It is imperative, as implicit in article 21, that life or liberty shall not be kept in suspended animation or congealed into animal existence without fair procedures. Fair procedure in dealing with the prisoners calls for another dimension of access of law-provision, within the easy reach of the law which limits liberty to persons who are prevented from moving out of prison gates."

"No prisoner can be personally subjected to deprivation not necessitated by the fact of incarceration and the sentence of court. All other freedoms belong to him – to read and write, exercise and recreation, meditation and chant, creative comforts like protection from extreme cold and heat, freedom from indignities like compulsory nudity, forced sodomy and other unbearable vulgarity, movement within the prison campus subject to requirements of discipline and security, the minimum joys of self expression, to acquire skills and techniques and all other fundamental rights tailored to the limitations of imprisonments."

"Inflictions may take protean forms, apart from physical assaults, pushing the prisoner into a solitary cell, denial of a necessary amenity, and more dreadful sometime transfer to a distant prison where visits or Society of Friends or relations may be snapped, allotment of degrading labour, assigning him to desperate of tough gang and the like, may be punitive in effect. Every such affliction or abridgement is an infraction of liberty or life in its wider sense and cannot be sustained unless Article 21. There must be a corrective legal procedure fair and reasonable and effective Such infraction will be arbitrary, under Article 14, if it is dependent on unguided discretion; unreasonable, under Article 19 if it is irremediable and unappeasable; and under Article 19 if it is irremediable and un-appealable; and unfair under Article 21 if it violates natural justice….."

The prison authority has duty to give effect to the court sentence. To give effect to the sentence means that it is illegal to exceed it and so it follows that prison official who goes beyond mere imprisonment or deprivation of locomotion and assaults or otherwise doing of things not covered by the sentence acts in violation of Article 19. Punishments of rigorous imprisonment oblige the inmates to do hard labour, not harsh labour. 'Hard labour in section 53, Prisons Act to receive a humane meaning. So a vindictive officer victimizing a prisoner by forcing on him particularly harsh and degrading jobs violates the law's mandate. The prisoner cannot demand soft jobs but may reasonably be assigned congenial jobs.

"The Prisons Act needs rehabilitation and Prison Manual total overhaul, even the model manual being out of focus with healing goals. A correction-cum-Orientation course is necessitous for the prison staff in calculating the Correctional values; therapeutic approaches and tension free management".

Human Rights in Correctional practices: Imprisonment as a mode of dealing with offenders has been in vogue since time immemorial. Though the foundations of the contemporary prison administration in India were laid during the British period, the system has drastically changed over the years, especially since the dawn of Independence. Apart from the native genius which finds its expression in the Fundamental Rights and Directive Principles of State Policy enshrined in the Constitution of India, new ideas and correctional practices in various countries have considerably influenced the texture of prison reforms in the country.

India shares a universally held view that sentence of imprisonment would be justifiable only if it ultimately leads to the protection of society against crime. Such a goal could be achieved only if incarceration motivates and prepares the offender for a law-abiding and self-supporting life after his release. It further accepts that as imprisonments deprives the offender of his liberty and self determination; the prison system should not be allowed to aggravate the suffering already inherent in the process of incarceration. Thus, while certain categories of offenders, who endanger public safety, have to be segregated from the social mainstream by way of imprisonment, all possible efforts have to be made to ensure that they come out of prisons as better individuals than what they were at the time of their admission thereto.

Objective of Prisons: As early as in the year 1920, the Indian Jails Committee had unequivocally declared that the reformation and rehabilitation of offenders was the ultimate objective of prison administration. This declaration subsequently found its echo in the proceedings of various Prison Reforms Committees appointed by the Central and State Governments of the international influences. The United Nations Standard Minimum Rules for the Treatment of Prisoners, formulated in 1955, provides the basic framework for such a goal. The International Covenant on Civil and Political Rights, propounded by United Nations in 1977, to which India is a party, ahs clearly brought out that the penitentiary system shall comprise treatment of prisoners the essential aim of which shall be their reformation and social rehabilitation. It is, however, seen that whereas India is second to none in terms of enlightened thinking with regard to the purpose and objective of imprisonment, the gap between proclaimed principles and actual practices appears to have been widening in recent years.

Rights and duties of prison inmates: It is, therefore, high time that in the light of observations made by the Supreme Court of India, the rights and duties of prisoners are clearly spelt out. In this respect, the All India Committee on Jail Reforms, 19801-83 has suggested as under:

Rights of Prisoners

1. **Right to Human Dignity:** Right to be treated as a human being and as a person; this right has been stressed and recommended by the Supreme Court of India which has categorically declared that prisoners shall not be treated as non-persons; Right to integrity of the body; immunity from use of repression and personal abuse, whether by custodial staff or by prisoners; Right to integrity of the mind; immunity from aggression whether by staff or by prisoners; Right to non-deprivation of fundamental rights guaranteed by the Constitution of India, except in accordance with law prescribing conditions of confinement.
2. **Right to Basic Minimum Needs:** Right to fulfilment of basic minimum needs such as adequate diet, health, medical care and treatment, access too clean and adequate drinking water, access to clean and hygienic conditions of living accommodation, sanitation and personal hygiene, adequate clothing, bedding and other equipment.
3. **Right to Communication:** Right to communication with the outside world; Right to periodic interviews; Right to receive information about the outside world through communication media.
4. **Right to Access to Law:** Right to effective access to information and all legal provisions regulating conditions of detention; Right to consult or to be defended by a legal practitioner of prisoner's choice; Right to access to agencies, such as State Legal Aid Boards or similar

organizations providing legal services; Right to be informed on admission about legal rights to appeal, revision, review either in respect of conviction or sentences; Right to receive all court documents necessary for preferring an appeal or revision or review of sentence or conviction; Right to effective presentation of individual grievances during confinement in prison t the appropriate authorities; Right to communicate with the prison administration, appropriate Government and judicial authorities, as the case may be, for redressal of violation of any or all of prisoners' rights and for redressal of grievances.

5. **Right against Arbitrary Prison Punishment:** Right to entitlement in case of disciplinary violation (i) to have precise information as to the nature of violation of Prisoner Act and Rules (ii) to be heard in defence, (iii) to communicate of the Decision of disciplinary proceedings, and (iv) to appeal as Provided in rules made under the Act.

6. **Right to Meaningful and Gainful Employment:** Right to meaningful and gainful employment. No prisoners shall be required t perform 'beggar' and other. Similar forms of forced labour which is prohibited as a fundamental right against exploitation under Article 23 of the constitution.

   Under trial prisoners volunteering to do work may be given suitable work wherever practicable. Such prisoners should be paid wagers as per rules.

   No prisoner shall be put to domestic work with any official in the prison administration; Such work shall not be considered as meaningful or gainful, even if some monetary compensation is offered.

   Prisoners shall, in no case, be put to any work which is under the management, control, supervision or direction of any private entrepreneur working for profit of his organization. This will not apply to open prisons and camps.

   Right to be get Wages for the work done in prison and Right to be released on the due date.

Duties of Prisoners

1. to obey all lawful orders and instructions issued by the competent prison authorities.
2. to abide by all prison rules and regulations and perform obligations imposed by these rules and regulations.
3. to maintain the prescribed standards of cleanliness and hygiene.
4. to respect the dignity and the right to live of every inmate, prison staff and functionary.
5. to abstain from hurting religious feelings, beliefs and faiths of other persons.
6. to use Government property with care and not to damage or destroy the same negligently or wilfully.
7. to help prison officials in the performance of their duties at all times and maintain discipline and order.
8. to preserve and promote congenial correctional environment in the prison.

Human Rights of Elderly People in Jail

Growing Members of Elderly Prisoners: One consequence of the increase in the length of sentences in some jurisdictions is that prison administrators are having to respond to the needs of growing numbers of elderly prisoners. In some jurisdictions the recent trend towards mandatory life long sentences has let to a significant increase in prisoners who will become old in prison. This may require the provision of a range of specialist facilities to deal with the problems arising from a loss of mobility of the onset of mental deterioration.

The Problems of Elderly People in Prison: Prison administrations will need to give particular consideration to the different problems both social and medical, of this prisoner. The growing numbers of prisoners in this category has led to the development of specialist units for the elderly in Indian, England, United States and in the other part of the world. Healthcare ends of this group of prisoners as per the Health Care norms of International Instruments of Human rights.

Composition of the Invalid Group (Model Prison Manual –BPRD): The invalid group shall consist of: Those who are permanently incapacitated from performing hard to medium labour because of age, or bodily infirmity. They will be the permanent members of the group; Those who have been discharged from hospital as convalescents, but are temporarily unfit to perform hard or medium labour; Men who are generally out of health even if not falling under the above two categories. This category shall include prisoners passed as fit for light labour only, prisoners exhibiting scorbutic or malaria scorbutic gums, prisoners found to be steadily failing in weight, and prisoners who are anaemic.

Treatment of the Invalid Group: Prisoners in the invalid group shall be given some light work suited to their strength and shall, as far as possible, be kept together for the purpose of diet and observation, both by day and night. A register of such prisoners shall be kept and no prisoner shall be placed in or discharged from this group without the permission of the Chief Medical Officer. They shall be examined daily by the Medical Subordinate, and once a week by the Chief Medical Officer.

Details of Prisoners above Age 60 Years
Central Prison, Coimbatore

Section	Convict	Remand
1	2	3
302 IPC	38	7
NDPS	3	5
379 IPC		2

1	2	3
376 IPC	7	2
307 IPC	5	1
395 IPC	1	
R.P.F. ACT		1
TNP. ACT		1
SC & ST ACT		1
420 IPC		4
480 IPC		1
506 PART II		2
NI. ACT	1	
IT.ACT.	1	
Total	**56**	**27**

Elderly Prisoners Conviction Particular of Central Prison Coimbatore

Section	Conviction
302 IPC (Murder)	38
379 IPC (Theft)	3
376 IPC (Sexual Offence – Rape)	7
307 IPC (Attempt to murder)	5
Other cases	3
	56

From the data of Elderly Prisoners taken from Central Prison, Coimbatore the following points could be observed:

1. Majority of the offences are took place because of the family circumstances like family circumstances like family disorganization, desertion, poverty and loneliness etc.,
2. Majority of the elders were arrested for murder of vengeance, murder for gain etc.

3. Next to murder cases the elders are involved in sexual offences.

Conclusion

Because of poverty, loneliness, desertion, family disputes elders are committing offences, Hence steps should taken to avert these problems right family level to society level. Elders should be treated with affection and security. Elders should not be deserted by their kith and kin. Government should also implement social security measure to protect elders from committing crimes. Government may provide them senior citizen allowances like in European countries. Like the olden days Indian community should follow our age old traditions like joint family system etc. Government may release aged prisoners under amnesty schemes.

Generational Gap

Youth's Attitudes towards Aged

— Dr. K. Nagaraju

ABSTRACT

The goal of this study is to explore the generational gap between young and aged people. The primary concern of this paper is to inquire the relations between youth's socio-demographic characteristics and their attitudes toward old age and elderly people. In this study social conflict between youth and old age is assessed through an empirical study. Data were obtained from the Coimbatore urban youths in Tamil Nadu. The research sample included 100 young people between the ages of 18 and 30 who were sampled for the purpose of analyzing and comparing their attitudes and perceptions of old age. The paper deals with the conception of old-age, value system, risk preference, presence of conflict and conflict management according to the gender of the young people. The study revealed that being urban youth, educational level of father, retirement from job and living in the same house have significant impacts on youth's attitudes toward old age. It is also found that there exists the generational conflict potential resulting from the risk perception of youth.

Introduction

The generation gap is and was a term popularized in the western countries during the 1960s which refers to differences between people of a younger generation and their elders. Although some generational differences have existed throughout history, because of more rapid cultural change during the modern era differences between generations increased in comparison to previous times, particularly with respect to such matters as old age, value system, risk preference, conflict and conflict management. This may have been magnified by the unprecedented size of the young generation in present century which gave it unprecedented power, and willingness to rebel against societal norms. The conflict between the generations has now reached an acute stage and is exhibiting itself in every walk of life with such frequency that an examination of its real nature, its causes and what means should be employed to reduce it has become a matter of urgency.

Broadly speaking, intergenerational conflict includes ageism. Blatant generalizations about older people are disturbing once we realize the great variety within the elderly population and the contributions made by seniors to our communities, especially in terms of volunteer work. However, ageism cuts both ways - many in our communities could easily fill in the blanks to complete these sentences "Today's youth is...." or "Too many young people think..." and so on. Ignorance about the variety and contributions of younger people in our communities is rivalled only by the same attitudes toward older people. Devaluing others is a source for conflict and does not contribute to creating healthy communities. It is unlikely that ageist behaviour and attitudes will stop as long as we maintain separate activities and separate lives for people from different age groups.

Intergenerational conflict is conflict between the generations which goes beyond the "generation gap" that families sometimes experience. It is conflict among groups within society; to some extent it is based on the attitudes and perceptions that older, middle-aged and younger people have of each other, and on the social values which shape and inhibit intergenerational relations. An important component of intergenerational conflict is the idea that different age groups think that they are in competition with each other for scarce social resources. This can be seen in a variety of ways. Newspaper articles claim the elderly receive too large a portion of public expenditures further ill treatment, physical assaults and even murdering of aged family members occurs in many places. Writers claim that social policies created to respond to the needs of older people in our communities create too big a financial burden for future generations.

As in our nation generation gets older - and they can expect to live longer than any previous generation - they will consume a lot of family as well as state services, especially social security and health care. That's another burden on the young because they lose job opportunities and are forced to take care of the ailing elderly. We will have an older generation spending its wealth to make itself feel younger, while the younger generation gets old before its time. The Age War has begun.

Although one of the most successful achievements of the modern times is assumed to be the fact that humans live longer (Wilson, 2000) old age is also defined as the latest field of social discrimination along with others like class, gender and ethnic based discriminations of the modern societies (Feagin and Feagin, 1997: 135). Furthermore in the recent days, as the human life gets longer aging is started to be perceived as a matter of generational conflict (Turner, 1998) rather than individual problem due to it's costs for the society both financial and social. According to Broer (2001) ageing leads to substantial increase of the tax burden and an estimated welfare loss for future generations. Moreover, inter-generational relationship has been elaborated by the studies of new dimensions of emotional support and care-giving, the impact of divorce and separation, changing roles within the family, narrative maps of ageing within the social gerontology (Shenk 2001; Scröder-Butterfill, 2004; Hyde and Gibbs 1993; Whenger and Burholt 2003, Keasberry,2001 Drew and Silverstein 2004; Phoenix and Sparkes, 2006).

Contrary to the former studies which are mostly focused on intra-familial cooperation between generations, Irvin (1996), Turner (1998) accepts Bourdieu's (1988) distinction between cultural and economic capital and formation of generational conflict. His approach assumes that there exists "distinction between individual aging as both biological and social process and generational conflict as structural aspects of social struggles over limited resources" (Turner, 1998: 299). Parson's (1962) sociological disengagement theory, which was widely used by gerontologists, was also criticized due to its failure to explain structure and stratification system of the society (Dowd, 1987).

In recent years, risk concept was elaborated by various studies in social sciences. According to Giddens (2002), in pre-modern times the relations with the society were based on traditions, relatives and local environment. The relationships of modern societies are ambiguous. The relations with the modern society are decoupled from the community, the context and expectations on how really they should be. In our days, it is the individual who is responsible for his/her own identity, either formally or informally. Everybody is expected to go along his/her own route in spite of the threats of the modern society and promises (Giddens and Pierson, 1998). For most of the young people, recent family structure and family relations are very different than in the past and it is constantly evolving (Jessor *et al.*, 1991).

According to Bartos and Wehr (2002), conflict exists wherever human exists: at home, among friends, at work and in societies. Because the human gains information about the conflict throughout his development. Therefore the methods that deal with the conflict are inherited from the family to the child. Bartos and Wehr (2002) state that the conflict has the same effects on the individual, group and organization. Even if the conflict knowledge is different from each other, they have some common properties. This is explained by the conflict theoreticians such as Bartos and Wehr (2002), Durkheim, Marx, Weber and Simmel. Bartos and Wehr (2002) first transform these theoretical assumptions to basic causal propositions and then to diagrams. They describe the possible reasons for the conflict behaviour in order to describe why the conflicts happen. There are six main reasons for conflict behaviour: incompatible goals, solidarity, organization, mobilization of conflict resources, hostility to the opponent and having effective resources. According to Bartos and Wehr (2002) the conflict behaviour can be regarded as a set of categories and process. There are two types of conflict behaviour: compulsive and non-compulsive. Non-compulsive conflict behaviour includes cooperation, rewarding and persuasion. On the other hand, compulsory conflict behaviour includes the threat of compulsion, violent compulsion and non-violent compulsion.

Indian population is known to be one of the largest youth populations in the world due to the high birth rate, but old age is also a problem especially in the urban areas of India. Therefore it would not be wrong to say that the research about the relationship between old people and young people is crucial one for India. Furthermore, increasing number of women has started to work in the labour market and this is resulted in the decrease in the size of job opportunities for families. Insufficient budgets and financial difficulties along with rapid changes in the traditional values make old people hard to live together constantly with their children, which mostly have the nuclear family form. Thus, as far as living space is concerned, there also exists discrimination between young and old people.

The aim of this paper is to discuss on 'old-age' from the youth's point of view. The primary concern of this paper is to inquire the relations between youth's socio-demographic characteristics and their attitudes toward old age and elderly people.

Objectives

1. To assess the socio-demographic status of the youths.
2. To know the youths' level of prediction about the old age.
3. To assess the risk perception and values of the youths towards old age.
4. To know the goals of youths and aged
5. To assess the conflicts between the youths and aged
6. To assess the level of conflict management mechanism adopted by the youths.

Methodology

In this study the researcher used descriptive research design. The major purpose of descriptive design is description of the state of affairs as they exist at the time of the study. Universe of the study is Peelamedu urban area in Coimbatore city. There are 18 wards in Coimbatore North from that Peelamedu ward was randomly selected. A survey was conducted to know the youth population following the inclusive and exclusive criteria. The total population was 643 youths. From them 100 were randomly selected for data collection. The research data was collected during November 2009 to January 2010.

Inclusive Criteria

1. The persons should be 18 to 30 years of age.
2. At least one grandparent should be alive.
3. The persons should live with grandparent(s) in the same house

Exclusive Criteria

1. Persons not having grandparents

2. Grandparents living in old age homes.
3. Grandparents living separately.

Results and Discussion

Most of the respondents (60%) are between the 18 to 22 age group. Nearly half (47%) of them completed higher secondary education. A high proportion number of respondents (72%) are employees in private organizations on temporary basis. Majority of the respondents (61%) stated that they are living with one sibling in the family. Twenty five per cent of them living with two siblings. It is noticeable that the education level of more than half of the respondents' fathers (57%) are restricted to secondary and higher secondary school levels. Fifty four per cent of mothers have an education level of primary and secondary levels. The finding shows that the education levels of the fathers are higher than the mothers. Majority of the respondents (86%) feel that the living space in the house is not sufficient for their family, so naturally the aged will get very meagre space in the house. It is observed that the aged has to spend nights in the porticos or common space used by the family members in the day time.

A high proportion of respondents (68%) state that they cannot predict how they will experience their old age. It shows that the youth population is uncertain about their old age. Majority of the respondents (72%) reveal that they are worried about suffering in the old age. The reasons are the problems of social security services and the risk definition may not go well as a part of modern social system. Eighty three per cent of the respondents feel that they should not depend on youngsters in their old age, further they reveal that some precautions should be taken to secure in the old age. Vast majority (91%) of them agreed that both youth and old have incompatibles goals. It shows that neither the aged nor the youth population has no proper planning about life goals. Majority (79%) of the youth state that the elderly people lack basic knowledge and hygiene.

More than half (56%) of the respondents state that they often quarrel with their grandparents for one or another reasons. The reason for conflict was aged people's interferences in their affairs and asked to do as they like, further they feel that misunderstanding with their parents will have its repercussions on non-earning grandparents. Majority (60%) of them reveal that the age old high values towards aged underwent changes, and also stated that the aged people lost their respect in the present society. Half of the (51%) respondents manage the conflict and find solution to the difference with the grandparents and also accept the persuasion of the aged. However, 39 percent of the respondents stated that conflict exists for a long time without letting it out, further they stated that it changed the phase and turned out to be open conflict.

Conclusion

Majority of the young people state that they cannot predict how they will experience their old age. A large majority state that they worry about suffering in the old ages. Majority of them reveal that some precautions should be taken to be secure in the old ages.

The findings show that the risk perception, strictly connected to the uncertainty thought, has an effect on the youth's judgments of old age. It may also be interpreted that family pension and health insurance will provide some security which has developed as an extension of this thought and works for the individuals feeling secure rather than being in secure, has been accepted by a vast majority. Majority agrees that the young and the old have incompatible goals. More than half agrees that the old try to persuade the young to behave as they do. That the presence of incompatible goals, which is one of the main factors of conflict, is widely accepted by the young verifies the presence of conflict between the young and the old. The reasons of conflict for the goal dissonance, which are expressed as competing sources, dissonant roles and dissonant values, may help the conflict exist for a long time without letting it out; if extra factors prevail, it may change the phase and turn the conflict into an open conflict.

The problems caused by a modern culture are solved in two ways: with violence or with dialogue. The young and the old should meet often and have dialogues and they should share a more social life. The meetings of the young and the old should not be limited to make them to interact. Social projects should be planned in which the young and the old work together in order to change the present negative information, attitude and behaviour of the young about the old age. Economic security and housing for the youths is essential to overcome the emotional outburst. Moreover, the relationship between the young and the old should not be limited to relatives; multipurpose centres have to be established in which the needy old and the needy young might come together. Social contact places and clubs for senior citizens should be formed for the old and there should be places for the young in all these centers. Educational activities and television serials should be organized with the help of the informative media means in order to annihilate the present negative information, attitude and behaviour about the old age within the society.

REFERENCES

Bartos, O.J. and Wehr, P. (2002) *Using Conflict Theory*, Cambridge: Cambridge University Press.

Bourdieu, P. (1988) *Home Academics*. Stanford: Stanford University Press.

Broer, D.P. (2001) Growth and welfare in an ageing society: An applied general equilibrium analysis for the Netherlands. *De Economist*: 149: 53-79.

Drew, L.M., and Silverstein,M. (2004) Inter-generational role investments of grandparents: concequences for psychological well-being. *Ageing & Soceity*, 24, 1, 95-111.

Dowd, J.J. (1987) Stratification among the Aged. CA: Brooks /Cole.

Feagin, J.R. and Feagin, C.B. (1997) *Social Problems: A Critical Power-Conflict Perspective,* London: Prentice-Hall

Giddens, A. (2002) *Runaway World: How Globalization Reshaping our Lives.* London: Routledge.

Giddens, A. and Pierson, C. (1998) *Making Sense of Modernity.* Stanford: Stanford UP.

Hagestad, G.H. (1998) A gray zone? Meeting between sociology and gerontology. *Contemporary Sociology*, 28:514-517.

Hyde, V. and Gibbs, I. (1993) A very special relationships: grand-daughters? perception of grandmothers. *Ageing & Society*,13,83-96.

Irvin, S. (1996) Age related distributive justice and claims on resources. *British Journal of Sociology* 47:69-72.

Jessor, R., Donovan, J.E. and Costa, F.M. (1991) *Beyond Adolescence: Problem Behaviour and Young Adult Development,* Cambridge: Cambridge University Press.

Keasberry, I: N. (2001) Elder care and intergenerational relationships in rural Yopgyakarta, Indonesia. *Ageing & Society*, 21, 641-665.

Parsons, T. (1962) Aging in American Society. *Law and Contemporary Problems* 27: 22-35.

Phoenix, C., and Sparkes, A. C., (2006) Keeping it in the family: narrative maps of ageing and young athletes? perceptions of their futures. *Ageing and Society*, 26, 631-48.

Schröder-Butterfill,E. (2004) Inter-generational family support provided by older people in Indonesia. *Ageing & Society*, 24, 4: 497-530.

Shenk, D., (2001) Intergenerational family relationships of older women in central Minnesota, *Ageing & Society*, 21:591-603.

Turner, B.S. (1998) Ageing and Generational Conflicts: A reply to Sarah Irvin. *British Journal of Sociology*, 49: 299-304.

Whenger,G. C. and Burholt,V. (2003) Differences over time in older people?s relationships with children, grandchildren,nieces and nephews in rural North Wales. *Ageing & Society*, 21: 567-90.

Wilson, G. (2000) *Understanding Old Age*, London: Sage.

Adolescent Identity Creation in the Midst of Grandparents

An Autoethnography

—Shilpa Thekkechangarampatt

ABSTRACT

Psychologists have marked adolescence as the most critical period in human development. It is a period of 'Quarter-life Transition' (childhood to adulthood). Parents, grandparents and teachers who directly involve in helping adolescents are confused and perplexed due to their unpreparedness to guide these budding personalities.

Adolescents get into trouble due to various reasons, mostly dealing with their family members, specifically parents and grandparents. It is because of the psycho-social development task of establishing self-identity that takes place in the adolescents (Erickson, 1963). Psychologist Erickson sees adolescent development marked by 'identity crisis' in which adolescents make a clean split from childhood to form an identity of their own. The recurring thought – I am not a child, I need freedom from my home; I need my peers; I want to do things in my own way – are some of the symptoms of quarter-life transition.

This study is an autoethnographic description of an adolescent seeking for identity living in the guidance of elderly grandparents.

The researcher uses self as the subject, presents a personalized account of the complexities, interpretations, and reflections towards creating what Erikson calls 'self identity'. Through an insider's point of view, using autoethnography qualitative research methodology, the study looks at both the positive and negative sides of living with the elders, facing the day-to-day problems and the generation gap experiences. The autoethnography research methodology felicitates in explaining the daily lived realities and the psycho-social development struggles through the personal experiences of the researcher.

Introduction

Psychologists have marked adolescence as the most critical period in human development. It is a period of ***Quarter-life Transition*** - Childhood to adulthood (Janetius, 2006). Many parents, teachers, and others who directly involve in helping adolescents are unprepared to guide these budding personalities. Adolescents get into trouble due to various reasons, mainly dealing with friends and family; include violence, parental problems, and gangs. Establishing self-identity is the main developmental task in adolescence. I am not a child, I need freedom from my parents; I need my peers; I want to do things in my own way: these are some signs of Quarter-life transition.

Erikson sees adolescent development marked by "identity crisis" (Erikson, 1970). Identity creation takes place in and through our social interaction. As we develop interactions with others, family members, outsiders, friends and other, a general question often raise in our minds: Who am? What is my place in society? etc. Often the adolescents are confused without any clear answer; an overall feeling of uncertainty about themselves and future trouble them. It is a crisis because adolescents make a clean break from childhood to form an image of their own. It is a process of adolescent growth where a balancing act between different aspects of the self, dos & don'ts, personal aspirations, the social structure and the environment and the reality of life makes one to think and develop who we are.

Here, role models become very important in establishing their identity. The major help expected from parents and teachers at this process of development is to provide them with healthy ***role models*** in their lives. Adolescent, who does not get a role model at this stage, in his parents or teachers in the school will sure suffer some identity problems in the process of growth (Janetius, 2006).

Methodology

This study is an autoethnography description of an adolescent's development seeking for identity. The researcher uses self as the subject, presents a personalized account of the complexities, interpretations, and reflections of an adolescent living with two elderly people in the house. Through an insider's point of view, using autoethnography qualitative methodology, the study looks at both the positive and negative sides of living with the elders, facing the day-to-day problems, the generation gap experiences and the elder's adjustment problems to old age.

This autoethnography narration is the self report of the author and her issues related to the growth as adolescent and the issues in dealing with the elders at home. Autoethnography is a recent qualitative research methodology which connects the personal to the cultural (Ellis, 2004; Ellis & Bochner, 2000; Chatham, 2009). Autoethnography focuses on the writer's subjective experience with a scientific outlook rather than the beliefs and practices of others. This study has been divided into three major divisions. In the first part the author describes the daily challenges that affect the identity creation. In the second part the developmental issues of grandparents with whom the author faces life challenges every day and in the final part the threatening crisis of identity creation.

Discussion

The Positive Side of Elders in Identity Creation: The elders give us a clear comfort zone at home. 'There is someone to take care of my needs and the safe felling that there is someone to guide me when I am confused and help me to look forward in the future'. This feeling of personal and social security put me at ease in times of trouble to boost my growth and development.

(1) Day-to-day challenges that affect the identity creation

(a) Disagreement among Grandparents on Daily Chores: Disagreement becomes a daily occurrence at home when adolescents live with elders. It is quite irritating when we see fight going on in the house between elders over trivial matters, like, why there is less salt in the curry and how the tea became cold etc. As a young adolescent, for me it is not a matter of discussion or quarrel for unnecessary things like food and salt. However, it is not so for them and that sometimes make me yell "Will the both of you just stop? I don't get up in the morning to listen to your yelling!" which is contradictory to my volume level. The irritation I feel is so high that I have the urge to shout even louder. But as far as they are concerned arguing and debating on small issues and concerns are their way of living and adjusting to the situation. I am too young to understand such day to day chores and constant arguments. I know that yelling doesn't solve anything. But I have to pitch my voice higher so that they listen to me. If I had said it in a lower tone, it wouldn't even reach their ears. They would keep on arguing as if I never existed. There would be silence following my outburst and then they would start muttering "See! The child is upset because of some other people!" so that the other could hear. Then the sparring match begins again. I just close my eyes and tuck all the irritation away, knowing no matter what I do it would all be futile.

(b) Imposing life style and the thought of living alone: I have talked to almost all my classmates regarding this point and blindly everyone says that this is the norm at home when there are elders. There are countless times I wish that I could live alone just so that I could actually hear the silence around me. But I do what I have learned to do best. The general complaints of the elders start from saying that I eat little because I don't eat huge amounts of food like others do. I don't need such huge proportions of food to sate my hunger. According to them, I am unhealthy, which I'm not. They then complain that I don't eat vegetables, but the truth is that I eat all the vegetables they give me and to them, being healthy means being fat, which I'm not and don't intend to become.

Another repeated grievance of the elders in the early morning would be: I don't read the newspaper or have any exercise. They conveniently forget the fact that first thing I do when I wake up I to walk in the courtyard with my dog and finish reading my newspaper then itself. They claim that I have no routine but in face I have a written timetable which I try to follow religiously. My dad has instructed me to have a timetable and I follow it. I get up at 6am no matter the climate and let the dog out. I walk up and down for 10-15 minutes, read both the English and local newspaper. Then I finish my studies and do all the preliminaries before I go to school. Although I am serious and systematic in my daily activities, following my own timetable religiously, still can hear complaints from elders that I lack routine, healthcare, daily exercise, and poor general knowledge. I felt ashamed often when I hear grandparents complain as if I behaved like a spoiled child. Imposing and expecting their lifestyle in me make me often think, "Am I an irritable baby, who makes a fuss when I don't get what I wanted".

It may sound as if I am making my own conclusions, but the elders seems to me more like a stubborn child than they think I am.

(c) Undue Interference in Privacy and Managing Friends at Home: One of the major things I expect as I am growing is my privacy and liberty. Many psychologists have also pointed out that freedom is the most important aspect of adolescent development. However, there are instances in which I used to feel that the privacy I desire is lacking at home. I feel that the elders are behind me to overhear my conversation which I have with my friends and classmates. Well, it may be the way of monitoring me as far as they are concerned. But for me it is so annoying that somebody is supervising me so closely at home that eats up my freedom. Sometimes the elders overhear partial conversations and make prejudiced comments without knowing what the situation is.

It also applies when my friends come home. As a way of initiating conversation my grandparents would keep on degrading my behaviour until it seems that I have no other job but to whine. This would create in me internal fear thinking, 'what my friends would think about me? Will not my friends change their positive opinion about me and my family?'

(2) Development of Grandparents

(a) Personality Changes in the Grandparents: A major thing I have noticed together with my won development at home is the development of my grandparents. We used to talk about everything ranging from the trivial and fun aspects to the mysteries and meaning of life. We used to agree on almost everything and we had such a great friendship between us. But as I grew up, I notice that they are more preoccupied with some kind of unfinished business or that sort. I see them growing and becoming more irritable and short tempered. The cheerful disposition and enlightening words that I get from them in my childhood seem to come rarer and rarer as days pass by. Their snide comments just leave me stunned as they would be totally out of context to what the conversation was. I can't imagine how much I missed the old conversations which we used to have until I would be at the end of my patience and close to spouting my anger. Then suddenly I remember that she has indeed become older and my anger vanishes.

(b) Fear of Death and Health Concerns: I know that I would give whatever it takes to keep my grandparents from being afraid of becoming old. When one of our relatives passed away with no health problems, the grandparents were shaken and the fear of becoming old as well as death is evidently noticed by me.

(c) Poor Handling of Loneliness at Old Age: Grandparents feel lonely whenever I leave for school, and that it becomes unthinkable about the time when I leave for college. They want to live in their world of small arguments and complaints. I know how lonely they'd feel without me but they don't see that I'd miss them too. It's a scary prospect to leave your nest once you mature but I have to go forward. I cannot stay forever here. I have to test my wings so that I could start my future. They think that my love for them is superficial and it wounds me when they throw that in the face. I want to leave for college happily that they have a life together and long and by cherishing all the good memories rather than wondering what mistake I did before I left. So I try to help them in all the ways I can. But if I help, it becomes an issue. If I don't help it is also an issue. So I am left floundering as to what I have to do. It wounds me to know that I cannot do anything. I don't know what their behaviour or reactions would be. When I try to lighten the moment with a silly joke, they take it seriously. They find fault in every little thing that happens. It is as if I have never had happy memories with them. All the joyous times I had with them, not grand or important, but the silly little things of everyday life, seem like vague dreams.

(3) Crisis in Identity Creation

(*a*) Lack of Appetite: Normally I would eat my breakfast with absolutely no appetite or taste and seethe. As my appetite is no longer present sometimes I give up the pretence of eating food and wash my hands saying 'I'm not hungry anymore'. They would start lecturing me and scolding me for not eating my breakfast and then continue to blame each other for making me lose my appetite. The sense of futility I feel at such times is so great that I would resort to anger. But there is no way for me to express it so it just churns inside me.

(b) I am Growing but Still Baby for Grandparents: As for my grandfather, he used to be cheerful and sunny all the time. Now his smiles and jokes are rare. The funny nicknames we used to call each other are long forgotten and the way he'd comfort me when I cry are long gone. Almost every day on the way to school, he'd make me doubt my own beliefs by telling me that I am only a child with no thought about the future. That is an issue with both of them. They keep believing that I am only a kid with absolutely no thought about the consequences of my choices whether it's about my education, life or profession.

(c) Anxiety and the Fears of Future: I'm not saying it's easy to live in an emotional roller coaster everyday and there are some days that I can't take any more and want to give up everything. But I remember all the great times we had and the love I still have for them. They have always been closer to me than my own parents and now they seem as distant as strangers. They know about my dreams and ambitions yet they remain stubbornly blind to my need to be something. I do have my own future to think of, my own job and education. They don't make my choices any easy as their actions force me to choose my own with doubts and anxiety. Life is not always about finding the right choice. But I do want to become what I am capable of and my love for them makes me want to find a balance between my dreams, my future, my parents and my grandparents.

Conclusion

Identity creation is really a struggle for adolescents and it is very true as far as my life is concerned. The conformations I get from my peers, classmates and friends make me think that I am not alone and all adolescents face similar problems in varying degrees and proportions. Often adolescents look for peer support, parental guidance to understand their identity and form their identity. Preparation for adolescent identity creation is a must as far as I am concerned; seminar/ workshops at schools and colleges are highly recommended to facilitate the growth and development of adolescents. Creating more awareness about identity creation issues would make the adolescents feel at ease at this time of confusion and turmoil. Good role models in the form of peers, mentors, teachers, parents and elders would solve a great deal of problems and help the adolescents in their identity creation.

REFERENCES

Chatham, C. A. (2009). "Do thyself no harm": Protecting ourselves as auto-ethnographers. *Journal of Research Practice. 6*(1). Article Retrieved April 17, 2009, from http://jrp.icaap.org/index.php/jrp/article/view/213/183

Ellis, Carolyn (2004). *The ethnographic I.* Walnut Creek, CA: AltaMira.

Ellis, C., and Bochner, A. P. (2000). Autoethnography, personal narrative, and personal reflexivity. In: N. K. Denzin & Y. S. Lincoln (Eds.), *Handbook of Qualitative Research* (2nd ed., pp. 733-768). Thousand Oaks, CA: Sage.

Erikson, E.H. (1970). Reflections on the dissent of contemporary youth., *International Journal of Psychoanalysis,* 51, 11-22.

Janetius, S.T., (2006). *Quarter-life Transition*. Retrieved on April 20, 2010 from - http://janetius.page.tl/Quarterlife-Transition.htm.

PART II

Transition from Joint Family to Nuclear Family and Elderly Concerns

— Binusha Joie

ABSTRACT

In today's world where joint families are becoming a thing of the past, the ones suffering due to the transition of the joint families to nuclear families are the elderly. Their lifestyle of having lived with the large family makes it hard for them to adjust to the new lifestyle of having to live with very few. Taking a look into the lives of elderly people who lived alone or with nuclear families can help us understand their problems. They face many problems which are overlooked or considered and their feelings are considered unnecessary. Loneliness is the most common and most serious concern that elders have when under transition from a joint family to a nuclear. After having lived with a large number of people, amidst all the hustle and bustle of a large family life, settling into the changes due to nuclear family lifestyle may be very hard. Loss of emotional support is another major concern. The lack of having people to give elders the emotional support they require makes it harder for them to overcome their problems and manage their emotions. Having no one to share their feelings makes them feel more lonely and also that they have no one to care for them. The security which the joint family provides is lacking in the nuclear family. As they grow older the need for security also increases and this is a major problem faced by them due to increase in nuclear family trend. As there are few people to give assistance to them, elders having physical needs face more problems. the feeling of inferiority when they have to be looked after or living on another members earnings, the loss of their 'leader' position in their large family and their lack of private space in a nuclear family and mainly loneliness lead to mental and physical illness. Suppression of feelings is also hard as they don't have many activities to keep them engaged and so have more time to think about problems. All this makes them feel they are growing older faster which has a negative effect on their mental and physical being.

Introduction

In today's world, joint families are a thing of the past. Nuclear families have become trendy and almost everyone seems to be following the trend. People don't have the time to share the joys and sorrows of their very own kith and kin. They move off to live in a world of their own. This reduces the love they experience as well as their ability to love others. They have time only for themselves. Their work, immediate family members and the very few activities done for the sake of providing themselves entertainment restrict their thoughts, imagination and expression of emotions. The working people or the youngster's of nuclear families may find it very convenient, but there are people who suffer due to this. They are the elders in the family. They suffer due to their way of living for the past years of life. Their small world would have revolved around their large families. A joint family would have been what they had lived all their life. When every family in the joint family decides to form nuclear families, the ones who suffer are the elders, the ones who had been the pillars of the family all the while it was young and till the family was standing on its feet. Once everyone moves out to form smaller families, they get left out with nowhere to go, no one to care for them and no one to share their feelings and problems with. The transition from joint families to nuclear families is a major source of concern for the elders. By taking a look into the lives of elders who had to live alone or with a nuclear family, a study on the problems they face was made. These problems make them a study on unhappy and mentally unstable.

Method

Direct interaction with the individuals who have undergone the transition from joint family to nuclear family and have gone through many problems duc to that has been followed. By looking into their world from their view, it has been easier to understand and come to know of their problems. Discussed below are the problems they face.

Results

The concerns of elders who undergo transition from joint family to nuclear family are many. They have difficulty in expressing their thoughts and emotions due to their age and mentality. But once they understand that they have understood that there is someone they can confide in, they have a lot to tell, including their problems, life experiences and about the ones they care for.

Types	Males	Females
Elders already undergone the transition	4	4
Elders in joint families	1	2
Elders in nuclear families for long period	2	2

Discussion

Facing Loneliness: The scenarios in joint families are completely different from those of nuclear families. There is someone or the other with everyone all the time. People hardly feel lonely in joint families. They share their lives with all their siblings, children and their parents. They experience a lot of love and warmth in joint families. This is something that can not be matched by any other love and warmth. Each member's problem or happiness becomes a problem or happiness for the entire family. Even leisure times are spent with everyone else in fun activates or just chatting away about the days happenings.

But when the elderly are put in a nuclear family, their narrow mindset makes it difficult for them to face the fact that they now have to live with very few people. Loneliness is the main problem that these elderly ones experience. The feeling that they are now no longer with so many people who loved them brings down their liveliness. The kind of loneliness they experience is something that they cannot describe. At their age and because of their mentality, they are totally unable to explain how they feel but can only cry, shrug shoulders, or make faces which speak for how they feel. The feeling of loneliness is the root cause of all the other concerns that they have. For them their world will have narrowed down to the very few people who they see frequently, and become very empty. The warmth of each member in the joint family is missed greatly in the nuclear family. The memories of incidents that took place and the moments of happiness that they shared as a joint family will be the only things keeping them company in their loneliness. This makes them long all the more for those moments again, making their loneliness more profound. This loneliness makes them pull away from other activities and from gatherings. They begin to assume reasons for which they have become lonely. They consider themselves guilty for small reasons which they feel would have hurt the ones who have moved away from them. These thoughts make them feel that they have been the reason for their loneliness. Had not loneliness been a problem, most of the following problems would not have existed.

Loss of Emotional Support

At home in a joint family, every member shares his/her life

with the rest of the family. The joys and sorrows of each member become the joys and sorrows of the entire house. During any time of crisis the elders who have to take responsibility, are emotionally supported by everyone else at home. The burdens of the problems are shared by everyone and so the weight of the actual problem on the elders is reduced. During times of loss of loved ones or anything of great value to the family, the elders who are most greatly affected are supported by the rest of the family. This reduces the pain and stress they have to go through. By sharing the problems with the rest of the family, they feel greatly relieved. The emotional support they receive from the family too helps them get over the problems faster, and also makes them more easily relieved. This in turn helps them think logically enough so as to find solutions to the problem. The children of joint families are usually not much affected during times of loss of a relative, as the elders are. At this time, the elders receive valuable emotional support from the rest of the family. The intensity of the grief is lessened with this comfort.

In a nuclear family, the elders usually do not have anyone to talk to or share their problems with, either they are alone and the only one they have to share their problems and feelings, may be their partner who is also elderly and may not be able to provide as much emotional support as a large family would. Or they may be part of a nuclear family of which now-a-days the members are usually working and so do not have time to share the problems of the elders. These people may not have the patience to understand the grief and sorrow the elders experience and so do not even try to comfort them in any way. This leaves the elders to bear all the emotional problems by themselves. the feeling that they have no one to give them emotional support makes them emotionally weary and prone to tears at the slightest provocation in such a predicament not only does the entire weight of their grief rest on them but also the sorrow that they now no longer have no one to support them emotionally heightens their sorrow.

No one to Share their Feelings

Emotions play a big role in every person's life. As emotions brew up, the more they are shared with others the easier it becomes to deal with them. Every emotion has its own effect on the person who experiences it. In a joint family, people are more open to sharing their feelings with others. Even if they try to hide their feelings someone or the other will be able to make out what has upset them. Happy feelings are shared with the rest of the family and this multiplies the happiness. Youngsters and working people are able to overcome or suppress emotions since they may have a lot to do and more of support from the society that they associate with. Elders tend to have few associates and so chances of having people close enough to them with whom they can share their feelings with are few. In a joint family the elders are sometimes comfortable to share their feelings with atleast a few in the family whereas they are not equally comfortable with their associates. The feeling that if not one person there is always another person with who they can share their feelings is also a source of comfort when confronted with problems. This is the positive side of being in a joint family.

When the elders are living alone as a result of others having moved away to form nuclear families, they have no one to share their feelings with except their partners, but this may not always be their best option. They have not much to do and so find it harder to suppress or overcome their feelings. When these elders live with a nuclear family, they sometimes try to hide their feelings so as to not let it show out or not to burden the family they stay with. Also they feel that expressing their feelings may seem like a sign of their weakness. The people in the nuclear family do not have time for the feelings of elders and also consider their feelings as unnecessary emotions. All this stops elders from sharing their feelings with anyone. Keeping their feelings to themselves create tension in them and also increase the feeling in them that they now have no one for them. The elders, as a result of not being able to share their feelings, grow more disturbed and are unable to think clearly or solve their problems by themselves. Feelings which were kept shut out from the world were what disturbed elders the most and this made them the hardest to understand.

Feeling of Less Security

The security which a large family provides is definitely not comparable with anything else. No security officer or commando team can provide the same feeling of safety a large family can. Elders lived in this sort of families all their lives. Even without their knowledge they would have had the sense of security within their family that they never experienced elsewhere. It would automatically be in the corner of their mind that for anything and everything they had people who they could rely on around them all the time. This not only boosts their confidence, but also makes them have a firmer stand in whatever they did. Being with many members made it easier to share the responsibility of keeping each member safe with everyone else. The whole scenario changes when they have to live in nuclear families or alone. They have no support with them. No one to stand by their side during times of trouble. This makes them feel less secure, making them less confident about their abilities. Doubt arises in them as to what they can do by themselves, which may surprisingly be the same things that they used to do all by themselves when they were with their large families. This may make them dependent on others around them or may stop them from fulfilling a necessity completely. These changes may be awkward or irritating to the family they stay with them, but only by understanding the change in mental situation of the ones suffering the major impact of the shift, can these problems be rectified.

Need for Physical Assistance

For those elders who have been in need of assistance due to physical inabilities, the shift from a large family into a nuclear family may be a large bang. The assistance that they received from many members would have to be shared now just by a limited number of members. This may make those few members find it a burden over a time to look after the needs of the elders. When there are many members, the work could be shared among them so that it would not come to them as a burden. As a result of the constant need to assist the elder, reluctance may develop in the member of this nuclear family leading to failure in assisting the elder. This can lead to many problems including strengthening of intensity in physical problems in the individual and the emotional problems which result due to lack of care.

Moving onto smaller problems which affect the elderly during and after transition into nuclear families, these problems are usually neglected or overlooked. But the impact they have on the mind, even though small may over time lead to serious problems. This would not only affect the elderly individual but also those who associate with them.

Too Worried about their Problems

Having more free time and being alone for more time in nuclear families, the elderly people tend to have more time to ponder about their problems. Having fewer people around them at all times gives them more time for thought. Problems which they would have put aside as a result of their ever busy lifetime looking after everyone else or just being busy enjoying the company of every other member in the family, will start being the only things they have to worry about in the absence of the other members. These problems which were once small and negligible to themselves seem to become bigger and bigger and eventually tend to take over their lives. Though this may seem impossible, by observing the lives of the elderly in such situations it will not be surprising to find them complaining about small problems. They also tend to find fault with small things that happen around them. All this makes them feel that there is nothing but problems around them.

This mentality makes them disturbed and anxious which as a cycle, results in more physical and emotional problems

Psychological Disorders and Physical Illnesses

Issues which may seem least important to youngsters or to members of the nuclear family, who are busy with their lives, may not be so to the elders who have to stay in these families. To them small problems may seem very large because they have nothing else to spend their time or worry about. Being too anxious may result in somatoform disorders or factitious disorders. Psychological disorders like depression, anxiety disorders are also common in elders who have to undergo transition from large families to nuclear families. The feeling that they now have no one around them to care for them is another factor which results in these disorders. the need for care and attention increases as age increases and when this decreases, psychological disorders and physical illnesses come up in their lives making life all the more miserable to the lonely elders.

Inferior Feeling and the Feeling of being a Burden

Being in a family where there are lot of members and having to head the family as an elder, would have given the elders a sense of superiority. Once the family breaks down to nuclear ones, the elders loose their position as head of the family. They then have to rely on others in the family to look after their needs. This makes them feel that they are a burden to those who look after them. Not only do they feel that they are a burden, but also a sense of inferiority fills their mind. The thought that they were once independent and now are dependent on others makes them feel small and low.

Unison in taking Decisions

For members of large families, decision making is usually not something that could be done by oneself. It was shared by almost everyone who was associated with the matter. Being the elder of a large family meant, having the largest say in the decision making of the house. Once the family is a nuclear one, the elders generally have not much say in the decision making. It is the family which takes decisions according to their convenience, sometimes even for the elderly. Even if the elders had to take some decisions, it would usually be for them only. This feeling of loss of place and stand can have a mighty effect on the mind of the elderly.

Loss of Leadership Position

In a house where a large family resided, the elder of the house was considered the head of the family. Decisions would be taken under the guidance of the elder and all activities in the house were done with their consent. This made the elder hold a position of importance in the family. After the transition into a nuclear family, the situation changes. Usually the family life is decided by the man in the family in accordance to the convenience of that family. The needs and view of the elder are not always given top priority in the case of nuclear families. In the nuclear family, the elders are generally dependant on the family with whom they stay and so they have to go according to their plans. For people who had been leading others for so long, having to listen to others in their old age may seem to hurt their prestige.

Feeling of Growing old Faster

Being alone and having plenty of time for oneself, makes them feel that they are now growing older. This makes them think of the limitations of the age. They tend to want to settle down to living a calm and peaceful life. This sort of lifestyle, according to them will reduce their needs and also stop them from being a big burden to the ones they stay with. As they lead this sort of life, the nagging thought of their age stays in their mind, in a way, reminding them of their limits. Doing this, makes them notice the signs of aging and it has a deeper impact on their mind. Elders tend to think that they grow in age faster than they actually are.

No Work to Do

For those who lived in large families, a busy life would have been a normal thing. Once settled into a nuclear life, especially for the elders of the family, they do not have much to do. Their life usually becomes monotonous. Having not many activities to do makes them unable to keep up with their past life. The energy which they used to spend on all the activities stays in them and this can make them very disturbed. Many elders who don't have much to do can be seen with illnesses, and many other problems mostly feigned by them, just to keep themselves busy.

Lack of Private Space

The elderly, who lived in large family houses, would have had a space of their own, mostly because it was their own house. After moving in with a nuclear family, it is usually seen that the elderly of the house do not get enough private space. Very few are fortunate to have their own rooms or private space which would provide them a little privacy. The elderly in nuclear families usually end up having to share the space with the children of the house or may have very little space for themselves. Privacy is very important for the elderly as they need to have space for their activities and for peace of mind. The need for private space for elderly is usually not understood by the families of today.

Conclusion

Problems that the elderly face just due to the transition from large families to nuclear families are too many to be faced by them in their aged world. Though they may seem small and silly to the rest of the younger world, standing in the shoes of the elders would give us a look into the intensity of their problems. By understanding their problems or at least doing something to reduce their problems will definitely make life much better for them in their old age.

Modernization and the Cultural Transition in India

The Elders as Victims

— Dr. Segar

ABSTRACT

This chapter is a comparative study of elderly people from two sectors, agricultural and industrial background. The main focus of the study is the urbanization and the situation of elderly people.

Change is the nature of human being. The changes that had taken place in the agricultural sector made tremendous change in the social structure too. As long as the agriculture remained the centre of the society, joint family system comfortably existed. Currently all over India, the agricultural sector is gradually decreasing whereas the industrial sector is increasing. The important factor of the industrial sector is migration to cities and urbanization. This leads to the decreasing number of joint families.

In the joint families, there are people to take care of elders. But in the nuclear family, such a possibility is not available. Due to the urbanization and industrialization, children study in the towns and cities and adopt the urban culture where as their parents and grandparents are not so familiar with the new scenario. Some of the reasons for the abuse of the elder people are:

1. *After the completion of studies children prefer for urban life; this could be due to job compulsions. But the parents are not ready to leave their native place.*
2. *The environment in which the elderly people were brought up is entirely different from their children. So, both the parents and their children fail to understand each other.*
3. *In some cases, the elderly people are not as adjustable as the younger generation to the new social values and changing culture.*

Consequently the parents havc to live away from their children. This leads to neglect and abuses.

Introduction

"All human beings are born free and equal in dignity and rights. They are endowed with reason and conscience and should act towards one another in a spirit of brotherhood." It is quote from the United Nations Universal Declaration of Human Rights, Article. Here it means that each of us is responsible to maintain human dignity and rights. But we fail to maintain this with our fellow men at large. The worst part of it is the failure to maintain within the family, with our own parents and grandparents.

We speak of human rights abuse at work place and at society at large but we fail at a time to notice the lot of things happening at home, around us, in our day today life. It is nothing other than the abuse of elders who are our own beloved grandparents or parents. We are to deal with others in the spirit of brotherhood. Today we are not even able to treat out own kith and kin with brotherliness, then how human rights can be realized in society as w whole.

The focus of the study is abuse of elders in their own families. It is a culture that is being adopted today that parents are sent to old age homes. It was a part of modernization in west. But it has turned out to be a fashion in India. Is it a blessing or a cure on younger generation? Are we deviating from the basic human values? These are the question to be asked by each of us personally. The social awareness has to be brought out on this issue. The condition elders in west are different from that in India. The Westerner has always been step ahead. They are used to live in privacy, and pay more importance to individual freedom. Hence many of them love to live in separate homes away from their sons or daughters. But Indians always love to live in family with people around; Indians give importance not only to freedom alone but also to duty. It is a culture with balance; Indians have been cherishing the rich tradition of respecting their elders, whether it is Mother, Father or Guru.

Indians are more emotionally attached to the family structure. But the last part of their life in old age home is a bitter medicine to be swallowed. Though it is bitter, many elders like to be at home because of the ill treatment by their family members. In West, many old age homes are taken care of by government. The elders are also economically independent when compared to Indian elders. But Indians are emotionally bound to their children and family; unfortunately their lives turn out to be pathetic day by day.

It was in the mid-1980s that erotological research, especially in the UK and U.S., began to focus on elder abuse. But more than three decades later, it remains an un-addressed concern in India, characterized by a lack of conceptual and definitional clarity. Since this crime is greatly under-reported, there is a lack of relevant data on it. The situation is complex by the fact that not all situations of elder abuse fit neatly into the existing legal categories. Hence many complaints that are made are not accepted. It is said that 80% of complaints lodged by elders are not accepted by police in Chennai.

Consequently, elder abuse as a social issue or as one that is relevant to public health figures very inadequately in the public sphere. This has resulted increase in abuses, family member forcefully take away the properties and sends the elders out of their living place. If appropriate interventions are made in this direction then in turn it could have helped in addressing the remaining unidentified problems of the elders. But there is empirical evidence to suggest that in India incidents of abuse and neglect of older within families and institutions, and that it prevails across classes, every state in the country and it takes place in both rural and urban settings.

There is also a widespread understanding that the neglect, deprivation and marginalization of older women are the normal consequences of aging. What is a particularly disquieting trend is the vulnerability of ageing women to oppression in various forms. Given existing structures of gender discrimination, women run a greater risk than men of becoming victims of material exploitation, financial deprivation, and property grabbing, abandonment, verbal, and humiliation, emotional and psychological torment.

Objectives

This study explores the current scenario of elders in and around Chennai. The elders of today have to face a lot of problems; so here, the concentration is on their present status of lives, material exploitation, financial deprivation, and property grabbing, abandonment, and verbal humiliation, emotional and psychological torment.

1. What is the root cause for increase in elder abuse?
2. What are the problems to be faced by elders today?
3. What are the remedies to this problem?

Methodology

The subjects of the study are elders at a Home for Aged, Chennai. The interview and case study methods are used to study the subjects. Most of the elders are from in and around Chennai.

The elders are interviewed with help of sisters who maintain the centre and also a case study method is used in some case to gather more information. An informal negotiation method is used for collection of information. There are 78 elders in the institute. The numbers of women are 48 and men 30. The group is comprised of two couples, two Anglo-Indians, two sisters of the same family, a mother and her daughter. The elders come from different economic situations.

Result and Discussion

The subjects for study are seventy eight. Women are 61.5% (48/78) and men are 38.5% (30/78) of the total strength. The educated members are 78% who were in good jobs (61/78; Male 24, Female 37) and 22% are uneducated (17/78; Male 6, Female 11). In that, 18% of elders are getting pension (64/78; Male 21, Female 43). 88% have children and they are well settled (69/78; Male 28, Female 41) but they were sent out by their own sons and daughters. Some others were sent out of home because they lacked the knowledge to live with their well educated modern son's or daughter's spouse. Few are out of home for the reason that there are no enough places to accommodate them. Some are out because they are a nuisance. Some of them are put out because they are a nuisance. Some of them are put out because they do not earn any more. The money and properties were forcefully taken away by their sons or daughters from many parents and sent out. It is only an effect of cultural transformation. Among them all only 11% are either unmarried or have no one to take care for (19/78; Male 2, Female 9).

Table 9.1 and Fig. 9.1 show that the average of sent out elders are much higher than the elders who have got no one to care of it includes both educated and uneducated members of the society. It also includes both pensioners and non-pensioners of the society. It simply means that elders are the unwanted members in the family.

Table 9.1 : Elder of Home for Aged—Little Sisters of Poor

	Elders	Edu-cated	Unedu-cated	Pension Holders	Non-Pension Holders	Thrown out of Home	No one to take Care
Male	30	24	6	9	21	28	2
Female	48	37	11	5	43	41	7
Total	**78**	**61**	**17**	**14**	**64**	**69**	**9**

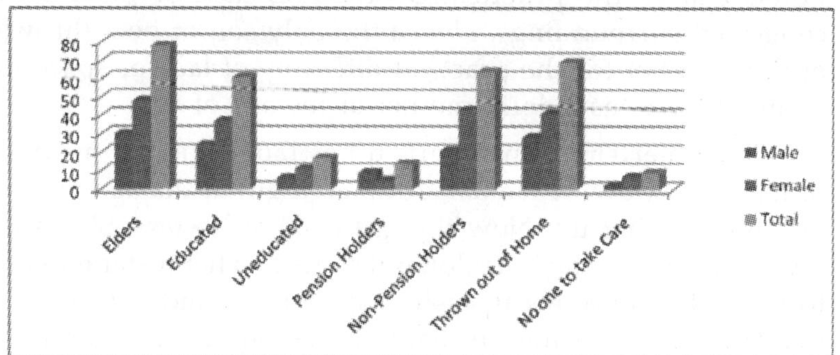

Graph 9.1 : Percentage-wise details of Elder of Home for Aged

Root Causes

It is necessary to analyse the root causes for this change in the society. The prime cause for this change in our value system is modernization. Modernisation has affected our culture and transformed a lot. One of most important change and is traditional joint family systems turning out into nuclear family. The joint family systems which were the back bone of our rich cultural values are broken away into nuclear families due to modernisation and mobility of labour. The characteristics of modernisation are intellectualism, individualism, alienation, consumerism, dynamism, workability, practicability, etc. These are the causes for value changes in a society and that led to the issue of elder abuse in India. To support the standpoint some cases fare highlighted from the study.

Intellectualism: The height of intellectualism is seen as a case where a son asks his mother to get out of house because she is not educated enough to relate with his friends and other associates of the family. Hence she was sent out by her own son.

Practicability: An importance is given to the practical aspect of life than other non-practical aspects. A son used the same measure with regards to his mother; her stay in the house causes the practical problem of lack of place and congested surroundings. Hence the only son of hers throws out his mother for the practical difficulty of lack of space to accommodate his elderly mother at the age of 68.

Consumerism: Consumerism has taught us the method of use and throw. A woman adopted a girl at the age of two and brought her up. Now the girl is an airhostess. She is in love with a man who is a pilot. But she asked her foster mother to leave the house because she would be a hindrance to her marriage as she wants to marry a person of high standard and her foster mother would be an object of degrade since she lacks modern culture. It shows her consumerist character.

Alienation: A couple have two children, one son and one daughter. But the children took away the property by force. Since the parents are sick and quarrelsome, put them out of the house. The nuclear family system has no much scope for learning the values like mutual adjustment and sacrifices. Hence the growth of intolerance is high to the level of not accepting ones own parents small and insignificant disturbances.

Individualism: Individualism has misled us into the direction that elders are against our individual freedom and privacy. Today one of the marriage conditions from the bride that parents of the bridegroom won't live with their son. A man sent out his mother because his wife is not willing to live with him. The height of individualism has taught him to be so selfish that he came to take his mother back when he wanted some one to take care of his child. When the child has grown up, the lady was sent out again and now she is back in the home. It shows that he is highly individualistic and selfish.

Hardship of the El ders

The hardships of elders are numerous. Many of them are emotional, hence the present laws are not adequate enough to safeguard and render legal support to the elders. Some highlight of the agony is brought out here.

Material Exploitation: Elders are the easy take for exploitation because they simply believe the sons and daughters. So this aspects turns out to be an easy exploitation, some tell their parents that they want to start a new business so they are in need of money. Parents always think of the welfare of their own sons and daughters and so they allow their son and daughter to sell even the living house, but in the end only they realise that was a trick by their own sons and daughters to get them out of their own house. Many even give away their pension and live in with the mercy of their own sons and daughters.

Financial Deprivation: Financial deprivation is another mode of exploitations. When the parents were earning all the money were taken away by their own sons and daughters and when they become too old and not able to draw any kind of income then they are to look at the hands of their own children but they never pay attention to them. The elders are given something by their children they have no preference in choosing or buy anything which they need.

Property Grabbing: Some of the survey has shown that abandonment takes place due to children and relatives greediness for the properties for the elders. So they tell the elders to give the property, if they fail to do so then they take away by force. The worst part of it is to throw them out of their own house. A couple who lived in the home had to face such a tragedy. When their children abroad returned and sold their house forcefully and went away.

Abandonment: It is one of main reason for the increase of old age homes. In the particular home, out of 78 elders 69 are abandoned by their own sons or daughters. It is 88.46% of the total members of the home that are abandoned and only 11.53% of the elders have no one to care of i.e. 9 out of 78 elders. They re under stress when they are sent out by their own people for whom they have sacrificed most of their life time. Many are sent out when they are sick and not able to take care of themselvcs.

Verbal Humiliation: Verbal humiliation is very common with many elders. The small mistakes which is committed by the elder due to aging is taken as a deadly crime and they get a lot of verbal humiliation, at times it turns out to be physical abuse also. According to *Malai Malar* in Chennai 23.2 % of elders are verbally abused and 3.6 are physically abused.

Deputy Commissioner of Police of **Mr. Sanjay Mohite,** in charge of the Social Counselling Cell of Mumbai Police says:

> *"Recently, I had to intervene in a case in which a young woman was beating and threatening her own mother, who had approached us reluctantly. I called the daughter to my office and told her in no uncertain terms that she should stop this ill treatment at once."*...this compels me to make this comment... *"When a daughter can beat and threaten her own mother then what makes one presume that she would not ill-treat her own mother-in-law that too when there is no law to stop her from doing so."*

Emotional and Psychological Torment: Emotional problems are much more painful than the physical ailments. There are no words for elders emotional agony. There are many sleepless nights in their life. So the sister in-charge of the house did not allow for formal interview because it might aggravate their longing and they would suffer sleepless nights.

These people have lots of psychological problems. They easily get depressed. Some start behaviour in a peculiar manner. So they are always under the care of well experienced counsellors. Whatever the amount of care and concern is shown, yet there is no permanent relief for their mental anguish/angry.

A couple who are living in old age home suffer personal humiliation to say to the co-elders that they live at free old age home because they had lived a dignified life and now their children are staying abroad. But their properties have been forcefully taken away and they are left alone. The old man gets a monthly pension and so they pay only Rs.40 monthly. He feels proud to tell others that they are paying fees and staying. They cannot give away their self identity and pride. So they feel proud in saying that their children are abroad.

Remedies

It is not so easy to prescribe remedies for elders' abuse. Many a time elders do not wish to explain their family issues with others. Even if they suffer a lot, they never come out to get of any legal help. Even if they are sent out, they feel that their children should live a happy life.

Modification in Legal Systems: The latest survey shows that Chennai is first in disrespecting elders, 71.4% of elders say that they have no respect at family. 56% of elders in Chennai do not live with their children either they live alone or in homes. 80% of complaints are not accepted by the police. 65.7% feel there is no use in complaining to police. 23.2% of elders are abused verbally and 306% are physically beaten. The reason behind all these abuses to the proof that the legal system needs a change. Many of the abuses against the elders are not considered wrong by our laws. such as material and financial exploitations by the children.

Proper Understanding of Value System: It is very much necessary to change the present materialistic value. People feel that the material things can give comfort. But many fail to pay attention to the emotional aspect. A son feels that his duty is over by sending money to his parents. Even many parents are not content with what they have, they want their children should earn more even if have to be away from homes for years together. Such kind of tendency has changed to value for sentiments and emotional into the materialistic needs and comforts.

Awareness among Elders: Awareness among the elders is a must. They should come out of the mere emotional and sentimental approach. They should understand the present cultural transition and should go for a kind of saving for them. They should not give away the savings at any situation. If they get any kind of threat because of such savings, they should approach the legal help and for that there should be a set of laws to help the elders.

Adjustment form Elder: Sometimes elders fail to understand the reality of present situation where both husband and wife have to go for work. So there will be no one to take care of them. They should think there is no use in demanding for love but it should flow spontaneously from the other side. So they should cultivate a new routine of life to find meaning.

NGOs and Government Help: They should act in responsible ways to help the elders. The NGOs can think of making awareness and proper counselling. Government can regularise the works of NGOs to carry out all over the India. The value education in school should not be a ritual and should be practical and the students of N.S.S and N.C.C can be properly regulated to help the elders.

Conclusion

The study would help in understanding that modernization and technological development have caused a considerable amount of damage to elders' abuse. The modernization is the cause for urbanization and the urbanization is the cause for the migration of the society. Hence the migration from rural to urban has become unavoidable in India. But it should not mean leaving away the values of respect for elders and their last part of life should be peaceful if not comfortable. The equilibrium between modernization and cultural transition must be maintained. Otherwise it would always result in problems. The individual freedom and privacy is necessary but not at the cost of elders being thrown into the old age homes. Elders also should not be driven by sentiments but should to understand the need of hour and act in accordance with it.

Startling Facts and the Torrents of Abuse

Does the health/wealth influence?— A Quantitative Analysis

— Prof. C.K. Kotravel Bharathi

"Old age hath yet his honour and his toil."

— *Tennysón*

"*A graceful* and honourable *old age is the* childhood of *immortality.*"

– *Pinder*

ABSTRACT

There is a common assumption that the elderly abused by the people around them quit their family setup and seek some other shelters which may be old-age homes or orphanages. It is also true to some extent. Some of the abused are roaming somewhere. But, apart from these people, there is another category that is consisting of the elderly who are often abused mentally or emotionally. They do not leave their families, but bear the signs of torrents caused by such abuse till the evening sunsets. This study focuses on such people.

Two sets of variables (i) The Startling factors (independent) and (ii) The torrents of mental abuse (dependent) would be taken into consideration for the purpose of this study. It would be also tested whether an extraneous variable called "Health and/or Wealth" is present or not.

The objectives of the study are: (i) identify the causes and nature of elder's mental abuse; (ii) analyze the impact of such abuses; (iii) test whether the health and wealth have an impact on the consequences of the torrents of mental abuse and, (iv) to analyse and offer the measures to avoid the abusive circumstances and overcome the consequences of such abuse.

The proposed study was conducted in three taluks of Erode District. A tool specifically designed and standardized for the purpose of this study was used for collecting the required data. The following statistical tools were used for data analysis. Cronbach's Alpha Testing (for testing the reliability and internal consistency of the data) Correlation Analysis

It is expected that the results of this study would bring out some interesting findings about the correlation between startling factors and the torrents of mental abuse. This study would further test whether the health and wealth have an impact on the consequences of the torrents of mental abuse. It would also give scope for the social work students, care-takers and organizations for the further extensive studies in this focused area.

Introduction

There is a common assumption that the elderly people who are abused by the people around them generally quit their family setup and seek some other shelters which may be old-age homes or orphanages. It is also true to some extent. Some of the abused are roaming somewhere. But, apart from these people, there is another category that is consisting of the elderly who are often abused mentally or emotionally. They do not leave their families, but bear the signs of torrents caused by such abuse till the evening sunsets. This study focuses on such people.

Review of Literature Olive Stevenson in his research paper published in the *'Journal of Adult Protection'* in February 2008 discusses the neglect of old people as an element of mistreatment. His study considers the definition and prevalence of neglect and issues arising both in self-neglect and in the context of professional and personal relationships. He argues that the underlying reasons for 'omissions of care' are various and complex and that distinction between 'intentional' and 'unintentional' neglect may be unhelpful. The evidence offered by his research suggests that it is the oldest and most vulnerable of elderly citizens who are most likely to experience neglect and that the numbers are not inconsiderable. This has thrown the light on the present study to focus on whether the elderly are neglected or paid due care in the geographical areas taken up for the study.

UNI, in the article entitled *"Message of Hope for 77 Million Elderly People in India"* published in June 16, 2007, states "Respect is better than food or drink. Almost one-third of elderly victims are abused in their own home and almost as many are abused in residential care. The most common type of abuse was physical, followed by acts of neglect or omission. In 20 percent of abuse cases, the victim was abused by a carer, partner or family member". This finding of UNI-Research provoked the researcher to test the state of elderly in his own home district by way of conducting the present study.

Shubha Soneja conducted focus group discussions in various parts of Delhi for her study on "Elderly abuse in India", which was given shape as a Country Report for World Health Organization. The sample was taken from urban society, residing in Delhi. Two major groups were addressed: the older persons and the primary health care workers who interact with these persons when they approach as patients.

Older Persons: Six focus groups were convened with the help of the author and an assistant facilitator in six different areas in Delhi. These groups comprised of members of senior citizens associations in local of residential areas of Delhi. The researcher further states "Discussions with male groups indicated that the middle income group listed economic problems on priority. The second male group from the upper middle class prioritized mental health problems focusing more on lack of work, lack of facilities for utilization of leisure time and a general feeling of loneliness talking to walls. The problem here did not seem to be lack of money but lack of time by the *others* for the older persons".

Dr. A. Mathur states that there is an urgent need to increase the awareness of elder abuse, neglect, and exploitation and to guide programs that protect older people. The ability of all professionals in the field of aging especially health and medical professionals should be increased to handle elder abuse. In order to prevent and decrease the incidence of elder abuse, neglect, and exploitation, dissemination of information on best practices should be encouraged along with development of special programs. Sustained endeavours and cohesive efforts need to be directed to accomplish this task in our country.

Conceptual Framework

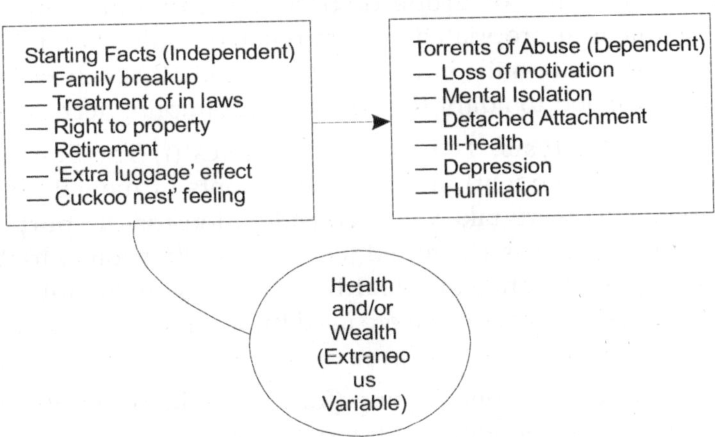

Objectives of the Study

1. To identify the causes and nature of mental abuse that the elderly suffer
2. To analyze the impact of such abuse on the elderly

3. To test whether the health and wealth have an impact on the consequences of the torrents of mental abuse
4. To analyze and offer the measures to avoid the abusive circumstances and overcome the consequences of such abuse.

Methodology: The study was conducted in three taluks of Erode District. A tool specifically designed and standardized for the purpose of this study was used for collection the required data. The tool for collecting data was consisting of 35 questions which were distributed as follows:

- Nine questions relating to the back-ground of the respondents
- Another none questions relating to testing of the extraneous variable
- The remaining 17 questions relating to the dependent and independent variables

The sampling unit consists of 120 senior citizens residing in various parts of Erode district. The random sampling technique is appropriate for more reliable results. But, taking into consideration the huge population and other constraints, it was decided to adapt the convenient sampling technique.

Data Analysis: Two sets of variables (i) The Startling factors (independent) and (ii) The torrents of mental abuse (dependent) were taken into consideration for the purpose of this study. It was also tested whether an extraneous variable called "Health and/or Wealth" was present or not. The following statistical tools were used for the analysis. The SPSS 16.0 was used for this purpose.

- Cronbach's Alpha Testing (for testing the reliability and internal consistency of the data)
- Correlation Analysis

Results and Discussion: This study has come out with some interesting findings about the correlation between startling factors and the torrents of mental abuse. This study has further tested whether the health and wealth have an impact on the consequences of the torrents of mental abuse. It would also give scope for the social work students, care-takers and organizations for the further extensive studies in this focused area. There were 47 males and 73 females among the respondents selected for the purpose of this study. 51 have been formally educated and 45 are pensioners. The age of the respondents ranges between 60 and 77. The data collected for the study were tabulated and analyzed. Apart from the simple percentage analysis, the following statistical analysis was also done for ensuring the effectiveness of the study.

Cronbach's alpha testing: Cronbach's alpha will generally increase when the correlations between the items increase. For this reason the coefficient is also called the internal consistency or the ***internal consistency reliability*** of the test. Cronbach's alpha measures how well a set of items (or variables) measures a single uni-dimensional latent construct. When data have a multidimensional structure, Cronbach's alpha will usually be low. Technically speaking, Cronbach's alpha is not a statistical test - it is a coefficient of reliability (or consistency). Cronbach's alpha can be written as a function of the number of test items and the average inter-correlation among the items.

α can take values between negative infinity and 1 (although only positive values make sense). Some professionals, as a rule of thumb, require a reliability of 0.70 or higher (obtained on a substantial sample) before they will use an instrument. Obviously, this rule should be applied with caution when α has been computed from items that systematically violate its assumptions. Further, the appropriate degree of reliability depends upon the use of the instrument, e.g., an instrument designed to be used as part of a battery may be intentionally designed to be as short as possible (and thus somewhat less reliable). Other situations may require extremely precise measures (with very high reliabilities).

Reliability Statistics

Cronbach's Alpha	N of Items
.722	14

Case Processing Summary

		N	%
Cases	Valid	120	100.0
	Excluded**	0	0
	Total	**120**	**100.0**

**List wise deletion based on all variables in the procedure.

If the Cronbach's alpha value is 0.7 and above, it will indicate a good amount of internal consistency and reliability of data. The Cronbach's alpha here shows a positive and encouraging value of 0.722. It shows that the internal consistency and reliability of data is good.

Correlation Analysis: In statistics, **correlation** (often measured as a correlation coefficient, **ñ**) indicates the strength and direction of a *linear* relationship between two random variables. That is in contrast with the usage of the term in colloquial speech, which denotes any relationship, not necessarily linear. In general statistical usage, *correlation* or **co-relation** refers to the departure of two random variables from independence. In this broad sense there are several coefficients, measuring the degree of correlation, adapted to the nature of the data.

1. Receiving Pension Vs. Treatment by the Family

The above table shows that there is a positive correlation between *'Receiving Pension'* and *'Treatment by the family'*. It can be inferred that the people who have the sources of income like pension are treated well by the other members of the family.

Correlations		Treated Well	Pension
Treated Well	Pearson Correlation	1	.585**
	Sig. (2-tailed)		.000
	N	120	120
Pension	Pearson Correlation	.585*	1
	Sig. (2-tailed)	.000	
	N	120	120

**Correlation is significant at the 0.01 level (2-tailed).

2. Level of Income Vs. Disrespect

Correlations

		Income	Disrespect
Income	Pearson Correlations	1	367**
	Sig. (2-tailed)		.005
	N	120	120
Disrespect	Pearson Correlation	367**	1
	Sig. (2-tailed)	.005	
	N	120	120

**Correlation is significant at the 0.01 level (2-tailed)

The level of income of the elderly people and the disrespect to the elders are positively correlating. It show that the people with higher income may be given due respect by the members of the family and the people with low income may be subject to disrespect. This happens when the income of the elders is not a greater support to the family or it is a very meagre percentage of the income of other members in the family.

3. Disrespect Vs. Ill health

The variables *'Disrespect'* and *'Ill-health'* are meaningfully correlating. It means the disrespect shown to the elders affects their well-being and they suffer both mentally and physically. If the same state continues, it puts them into a highly depressed condition.

Correlations

		Ill health	Disrespect
Ill health	Pearson Correlation	1	.639**
	Sig. (2-tailed)		.000
	N	120	120
Disrespect	Pearson Correlation	.639**	1
	Sig. (2-tailed)	.000	
	N	120	120

**Correlation is significant at the 0.01 level (2-tailed)

4. Feeling Happy about Joint Family Vs. Good Health

Correlations

		JF Happy	Good health
JF Happy	Pearson Correlations	1	.556**
	Sig. (2-tailed)		.005
	N	120	120
Good health	Pearson Correlation	.556**	1
	Sig. (2-tailed)	.000	
	N	120	120

**Correlation is significant at the 0.01 level (2-tailed)

There is always an association between the physical well-being and mental well-being. The above analysis show that there is a strong positive correlation between *'Feeling happy about the joint family'* and the *'Good health'* of the elders. This can be inferred that the elders who feel so happy about the healthy state of their joint family are blessed with good health.

5. Correlation between Gender and Other Variables

Correlations

		Gender	Education	God Affection	Heirs Good
Gender	Pearson Correlations	1	432**	359**	481**
	Sig. (2-tailed)		.001	.006	.000
	N	120	120	120	120
Education	Pearson Correlation	432**	1	.092	.066
	Sig. (2-tailed)	.001		.495	.626
	N	120	120	120	120
Gnd Affection	Pearson Correlations	359**	092	1	408**
	Sig. (2-tailed)	.006	.495		.002
	N	120	120	120	120
Heirs Good	Pearson Correlation	.481**	0.66	408**	1
	Sig. (2-tailed)	.000	.626	.002	
	N	120	120	120	120

**Correlation is significant at the 0.01 level (2-tailed)

The above analysis shows that the variable *'Gender'* is positively correlating with the other three variables *'Education'*, *'Affection of the grand children'* and *'Good treatment by the heirs'*. It is interesting to note these associations. Among the respondents selected, most of the female are not educated or little educated. So, it is reasonable to have the correlation between gender and education. But it seems to be peculiar to note that the correlation between *'Gender'* and *'Affection of the grand children'*. But we can find the appropriate reason if we further probe into this issue.

Conclusion

The present study reveals that there are cases of the elders who suffer because of the abusive situations in the family. If we again and again analyze the torrents that are left in the lives of the elderly due to the abusive situations and incidents, we can find the startling facts behind those torrents.

Anyhow the people with good health or good sources of income do not suffer much due to the torrents of abuse. This is also revealed by this study. So, we cannot blindly say that all the startling facts (independent variables) taken up for this study will surely result in the torrents of abuse (dependent variables). The existence of the extraneous variable 'Health and/or Wealth' is proved in this context. Hence, the relationship between the dependent and independent variables has become confounded. But this finding is applicable to the conditions prevailing in the context of this study only. This cannot be generalized to the entire society.

Scope for Further Studies

This study provides scope for further studies in analyzing the torrents of abuse. If this study is carried on at a large basis in various districts throughout the state and at national level, it may come out with different and more authenticated findings. The same study may be conducted exclusively at various sectors of the society and at various social-classes. The results of such exclusive studies may lead to a concrete comparative analysis also.

The couplet-892 of the greatest Tamil Scripture *'Thirukkural'* written by the Tamil Poet Thiruvalluvar says *"Those who behave without respect for the great elderly people will suffer from irremediable evils"*. If the values insisted by such scriptures are firmly instilled in the minds of every one, there will be no question of abuse of elders.

Abuses faced by Elderly in Family

A Micro Study in Unpaid Aged Homes

– Thanuja Thomas

ABSTRACT

Abuses on the elderly people are on the increase. Elder abuse tends to take place where the senior lives, most often in their own homes as well as in the aged homes. In this micro study the researcher attempts to find out the different forms of abuse faced by elderly and perpetrators of elder abuse and their personal and family condition of the 200 elderly persons in different unpaid old age homes in Kottayam district in Kerala.

The research design was descriptive and the researcher collected data through individual interview method and adopted a purposive sampling technique. Data analysis shown that the majority of the inmates faced some form of abuse before they enter into the old age homes and majority of the perpetrators were daughter-in-laws.

Introduction

Abuse or mistreatment of the elderly is not a new phenomenon. But it came in to focus only during 1970 and

1980s. In India the elderly population still depends heavily on the family for economic and emotional support. Joint living with sons seems to be the predominant form of living arrangement of the elderly.

Further, it is predicted that India would reach the threshold level of Net Reproductive Rate (NRR) of one child per family within a decade or so. As we are entering a model family situation where fewer children would be available for sharing the responsibility of care for the elderly parents, the likelihood of neglect and abuse of the elderly also increases.

Elder abuse refers to a wilful mistreatment and neglect. Mistreatment is an act of commission, while neglect is an act of omission. The mistreatment can be physical, psychological, social or of miscellaneous types. Wilful neglect, deprivation of the elders' normal privileges, and exploitation also constitute mistreatment.

Abuse is a pattern of behaviour that results in physical or psychological harm. It is of many types for example include verbal abuse, intimidation, threats of placement in care, withholding affection, treatment of older people like children, economic abuse - improper use of their money and property, physical assault or restriction of their movement, neglect both active and passive, and dependency issues which can lead to stress and abuse.

More women than men are abused, especially if the person is a widow, and there is no one to protest. Gender, Illiteracy and absence of financial resources make her totally dependent on her son and daughter in law to pass their final days of their life. They are tied to the family for emotional reasons, rationalizing the behaviour of their children, believing that such a treatment is a matter of destiny, or that there must have been some lapses in the upbringing of their son which has made him hostile, and/or entirely submissive to the daughter in law's attitude.

Thus, in view of the problems faced by the elderly in the changing family context, the elder abuse and neglect becomes a topic of significant interest and focus for researchers, social workers and policy makers.

The daily news article revealed that elderly persons in India face more abuse by their own family members than by those outside home. And, sons and daughter-in-law are the main abusers at home. These are the findings of a study on elder abuse in India conducted by Help Age India, in eight cities. One-third of the elderly persons faced abuse over property. But rarely do they complain to the police. About 14 percent faced physical abuse. Over 40 percent of the older people complained they were disrespected and they considered this as abuse. Another nearly 40 percent faced verbal abuse. Neglect, economic abuse and emotional abuse were other abuses.

The news article reveals that Kerala, which has the largest number of old people aged above 60, also has the dubious distinction of harassing them the most. Worse, the abuse is being meted out by their children or grandchildren who want to avoid them in times of need. The revelations were made by an ongoing survey by the Centre for Gerontological Studies (CGS) here commissioned by the Centre. Centre chairman P K B Nayar told *Deccan Herald* that the survey, which is halfway through, has found that a large section of the elderly in the state are being subjected to mental and physical abuse. Kerala, known for its high health indices, has the largest number of elderly people—about 10 per cent of the population. Not surprisingly, it also has a large number of old age homes compared to other states. According to the survey, old parents were either deprived of proper food, clothes, adequate medical attention, and proper accommodation or ignored altogether.

Various forms of abuses of abuse could be classified as follows:

1. Neglect: A more prevalent form of abuse is neglect. Essential needs of older persons are not met, or are treated in a casual manner. These may relate to confining the person to the home, not helping him to go out and interact with neighbours and friends, or to consult with a doctor.

2. Psychological or Mental abuse: Psychological or mental abuse of older persons which causes them stress, lowers their dignity and self worth, and is extremely disturbing. Direct insulting behaviour, harsh language, yelling, imitating or making fun, passing caustic remarks, humiliating conduct and treatment, totally ignoring them in interpersonal contacts within the family, with restraining contacts with relatives and neighbours, and socially isolating them.

3. Physical Abuse: It could result in hurting or injuring the older person, hitting the person, handling the person roughly, causing pain or temporary impairment, causing fear, or physically restraining movement. It could also imply the deliberate use of medication to keep the person quiet.

4. Financial Abuse: Various methods are used such as neglect, threats, harassment, taunts, caustic remarks and abusive conduct to compel the person to give away the property. Retirements benefits are at times taken away by a son to buy a house in his name, assuring the person of care and comfort. Unauthorized or fraudulent use of the person's money, property or other financial resources, forging of signatures ,abuse of power of attorney, disposal of property or cash using deceit, trickery or force, pressurizing the person to make a will in their favour, or change the will or other legal documents.

5. Other forms of Abuse: Denying elder's sexuality, telling elders what to wear, refusing to respect their privacy, arranging physical surroundings to suit institutional priorities, preventing social interaction with others belittling older people in any manner; undermining their confidence, and disparaging other family members.

Objectives

- To study the Personal and family condition of the respondents.
- To know the abuses faced by the respondents before enter in to the old age home.
- To know the perpetrators of elderly abuses
- To give suggestion to create social awareness.

Methodology: The research design adopted by the researcher was descriptive. Kottayam district in Kerala was selcected randomly from the 14 districts of Kerala State. In Kottayam there are 23 free homes, from which the researcher purposively selected only 8 free homes for the study. The total population in unpaid home was 341 (male 140 female 201) of which 200 respondents are randomly selected. Inmates those who are not willing, bedridden and those who have Psychiatric problems were not taken for this study. The researcher has prepared interview schedule and used interview method for data collection.

Results and Discussion: Majority of the respondents (35%) belong to 76 year and above age group, it shows the health status and longevity of the elderly population in Kerala was higher than the national average. 55.5 per cent of the respondents were females. It shows the longevity of the female persons and also Kerala state general population the female ratio outnumbered the male. More than half (55 per cent) of the respondents belong to the Christian religion. In Kottayam district majority of the general population belong to Christians and majority (62.0 per cent) belong to forward community. Nearly half (45.5 per cent) of the respondents were married, 38.5 per cent of them were single persons. Majority (61.5 per cent) of the respondents belongs to nuclear family. Majority (46.5 per cent) studied up to 5th standard (Kottayam district is occupied most literate people compare to any other district in India). 44.5 per cent of the respondents (female) previous occupation was housewives and 24.5 per cent of them were coolies. More than one-third (36.5%) of the respondent had one to two child, 21.5 per cent of them had three and more child. Whereas 27.5 per cent of them were childless and remaining 14.5 per cent of them were single. Majority (72.5%) of the respondents financial background was poor, as we know that the majority of the Indian elderly persons are living below poverty line. General health condition of the respondent was satisfactory because of increased medical facilities and reduced morbidity rate. Majority (67.5%) of the respondents joined the institution because of familial and financial problem. Majority (78.5%) of the respondents felt that their current living arrangement is good and 45.5 per cent of them would like to continue their life in institution than living with children (17.0 per cent) or in their own home (37.5%). More than half (54.0%) of the respondents suffered psychological or emotional abuse from their family. Majority (64 per cent) of the perpetrators were daughter in laws. In India majority of the elderly persons living with their married sons, so it cause more stress on daughter-in-laws than elderly persons own children. Especially if the daughter in-law is working woman the stress and burden will be multiplied, and it leads to elderly abuse or ill-treatment.

Recommendations

A few concrete steps must be taken to change this situation. Screening programmes in communities to identify the problem families and older people who are at risk of abuse and neglect. Educational programmes for victims of abuse to provide information about their rights and steps they can take to reduce the risk of being abused or neglected. Mixing old and young in community programmes, Create their own (Elderly) support system are some easy ways to make people aware of the problem. Socializing the elderly with the outside community programmes is an important strategy to prevent elder abuse and neglect in society. Stress management training programmes for care givers, Support from other potential care givers may reduce the abuse. Victims are offered and provided with counselling and assistance to empower to confront different situations and enjoy freedom.

Conclusion

The Indian population is ageing faster, it is therefore unrealistic to expect, in the light of the current socio-economic scenario, either the family to completely take care of the elderly or the government to subsidise the elderly care programmes any longer. It is time now to think of viable alternatives to supplement the family care giving and to replace the other institutional arrangements, so that the older people can lead a life of dignity free from exploitation and neglect. Abuse of elder person is on the increasing trend. The incidence is grossly under reported as it is considered as an intra family matter, not to be communicated to outsiders so that the dignity of the family can be maintained. This attitude perpetuates its recurrence. There is an urgent need to generate public awareness of the emerging problem of abuse and to initiate steps to alleviate the problem.

REFERENCES

Bose, A.B. (2006) *Social security for the old—Myth and Reality*, Concept Publishing Co. Ltd, pp. 226-232.

Desai, Amith & Siva Raju (2000) *Gerontological Social work in India*—Some issues and Perspectives, B.R. Publishing Co., pp. 219-234.

Domunelli, Lena (2004) *Social work—Theory and Practice for a Changing Profession,* Polity Press, UK, p. 20. Jamuna, D. (2003) Journal of Aging & Social Policy, Vol. 15(2/3), 2003 , p. 135.

Koradia, Dr. Kavita, Rikhita Singhal, Dr.Darshan Narang (2009), Empowering elderly against abuse and crime, Abstract and papers of *International Conference on "Multidisciplinary Approach to Healthy and Participatory Ageing"* conducted by S.N.D.T women's university, S.V.T college of Home Science, Mumabai, pp. 249-251.

Financial Abuses of the Elderly

— R. Ransom Ruth Hephzibah

— Dr. V. Darling Selvi

ABSTRACT

Elder abuse is an age old story. It happens everywhere, at homes, at our neighbourhood and at care centres. It can happen anywhere were there are older people who have a difficult time advocating for or defending themselves and their rights.

Denying any individual their personal safe or their rights becomes an abuse. When we talk about financial abuse, mishandling someone's personal finances is the primary abuse we can talk about. The Administration on Aging in America defines elder abuse as follows: "Elder abuse is an umbrella term referring to any knowing, intentional, or negligent act by a caregiver or any other person that causes harm or a serious risk of harm to a vulnerable adult." Elder abuse is a general term used to describe certain types of harm to older adults. This study in an attempt of analyzing the financial difficulties met by the elderly population at home and in society.

The data were collected by the researcher through a well prepared an interview Schedule among fifty elders in Kanyakumari District.

Statistical tools like Yeles's Coefficient of Association, percent analysis and the like are applied to bring fruitful results. The researcher concluded that proper financial security with viable investment will help the elders to regain their financial and social status.

Introduction

The official statistics reveal that large segments of the elderly in India are illiterate, out of work force, partially or totally dependent on others and suffering from health problems or physical disabilities. The only welfare measure for the elderly considered by the government until the Seventh Five-year Plan was the running of old age homes. The Eighth and Ninth Plans, however, incorporated fairly more specific and comprehensive welfare measures for the elderly such as provision of old age homes, day care centres, Medicare and non-institutional services. The Government of India is committed to provide an effective environment to secure the goals of economic and emotional security for the elderly. It also recognizes that all institutions of civil society, individuals and the community at large are equal and effective partners in securing that goal.

India is witnessing a demographic transition, leading to a rapid increase in the number of older people. A child born 60 years ago in India had an average life expectancy at birth of 32 years, whereas a child born in 2007 is expected to live 64 years and longevity is expected to enhance further. India had the second largest number of elderly (60+) in the world as of 2001, gradually swelling up from 24 million in 1961 to 77 million in 2001. Elderly persons in India are likely to constitute 17.5% of the population in 2050 from 7.5% in 2001. The success story of increasing longevity in India is now creating a new challenge for ensuring the well-being of the enormous number of the elderly.

Table 12.1 : Population of the Elderly

Year	Number (million)	Trend %
1901	12	100
1951	20	167
1981	42.5	354
1991	57	475
2001	77	642
2013	100	833
2016	103	858
2021	137	1142
2030	198	1650
2050	326	2717
Average	107	894

Source: Compiled from the Census Reports.

The population of elderly is growing fast as it is evident from Table 12.1. By taking 1901 as the base year, the trend is

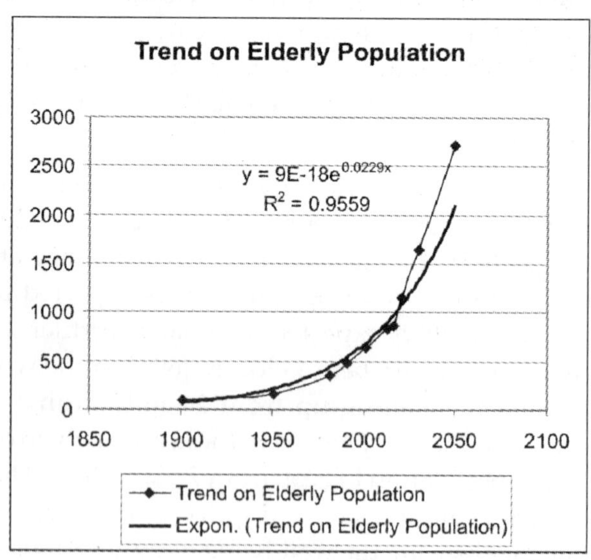

Fig. 12.1.

calculated and it shows an increasing rate of 542 per cent during 2001 and the same is projected to be increased 2617 per cent in the year 2050. The average growth rate is 794 per cent over the years under study. The trend line is sloping upwards with an exponential growth rate of 22.9 per cent and .96 as the coefficient of determination.

Table 12.2 : Population by Broad Age Groups

Age group	Kanyakumari District ('000)	Tamil Nadu ('000)	Percent to total	
			District	State
0-14	419	16826	25	27
15-19	174	6087	10	10
20-24	166	5917	10	9
25-29	154	5520	9	9
30-34	125	5038	8	8
35-39	123	4610	7	7
40-44	101	4054	6	6
45-49	102	3480	6	6
50-54	78	2889	5	5
55-59	67	2349	4	4
60-64	54	1940	3	3
65-69	43	1468	3	2
70-74	31	1130	2	2
75-79	19	686	1	1
80 and above	20	441	1	1
Total	**1676**	**62406**	**100**	**100**

Source: Census of India 2001.

As per the census of India 2001, it is known that the combination of ageing in Tamil Nadu and the study area Kanyakumari District is given in Table 12.2 above which reveals that 10 per cent people in Tamil Nadu and 9 per cent people in Kanyakumari District have crossed the age of 60 and have considered as senior citizens.

Table 12.3 : Aged Population of Kanyakumari District

Population	Senior Citizens	
	Number (million)	%
16,67,763	1,67,909	10.05
Male	83924	50
Female	83985	50
	Age group	
60 – 64	52260	32.32
65 – 69	43808	26.09
70 – 74	31083	18.51
75 – 79	18354	11.04
Above 80	16813	10.36

Source: Census of India 2001

The total population of the district is 16, 67,763. Among them, 10.05 per cent represents senior citizens i.e. 1, 67,909 (males 83924 and females 83985). 32.32 per cent of the total older population (52260) is in the age group of 60–64, the age group 65–69 consists of 43808 (26.09 per cent of the total older population) and 31083 (18.51%) are in the age group of 70–74. 18354 (11.04%) belong to the age group of 75–79. The number of senior citizens above 80 is 16813.

Elder abuse: Elder abuse is dark and ugly. It happens in residential centres, at home, in neighbour's family, in medical facilities. It can happen anywhere there are older people who have a difficult time advocating for or defending themselves and their rights. Abuse of older people is not limited to dementia patients. It doesn't only happen to extremely old people, and it is not limited to physical abuse. Denying any individual their personal safety or their rights is abuse. Mishandling someone's personal finances is abuse. Neglect is, too. Elder abuse is a general term used to describe certain types of harm to older adults. Other terms commonly used include: "elder mistreatment", "senior abuse", "abuse in later life", "abuse of older adults", "abuse of older women", and "abuse of older men". One of the more commonly accepted definitions of elder abuse is "a single, or repeated act, or lack of appropriate action, occurring within any relationship where there is an expectation of trust which causes harm or distress to an older person." This definition has been adopted by the World Health Organization from a definition put forward by Action on Elder Abuse in the UK. The Action on Elder Abuse (AoA) defines elder abuse as "Elder abuse is an umbrella term referring to any knowing, intentional, or negligent act by a caregiver or any other person that causes harm or a serious risk of harm to a vulnerable adult." A survey which has been conducted among 25 elder people in Kanyakumari District during the month of June 2010 has revealed the following results with regards to their various forms of abuses.

Table 12.4 : Personal Profile of the Sample Respondents

Variables	Frequency	Per cent	Cumulative Per cent
1	2	3	4
Age			
60-65	6	24	24
66-70	7	29	53
71-75	3	12	65
76-80	6	24	89
81-85	3	12	100
Total	25	100	
Sex			
Male	10	40	40
Female	15	60	100
Total	25	100	
Employment after retirement			
Yes	2	8	7
No	23	92	100
Total	25	100	

1	2	3	4
Qualification			
School	13	50	50
Degree	9	38	88
PG	3	12	100
Total	25	100	
Occupation			
Retired	17	69	69
Housewives	8	31	100
Total	25	100	
Spouse			
Living	23	93	93
Expired	2	7	100
Total	25	100	
Mode of living			
Single	3	12	12
Family	20	80	92
Old age homes	2	8	100
Total	25	100	
No. of dependents			
Nil	20	80	80
1-3	5	20	100
Total	25	100	

Source: Primary Survey

The survey (Table 12.4) shows that 53 percent of the sample respondents' fall below the age group of 70, 36 percent between 71 and 80 and the rest 12 per cent between 81 and 85, 40 per cent male members and 60 per cent female members, and only 8 per cent have reemployed after retirement. Among them, 50 per cent have completed their school education only, 38 per cent degree holders and 12 per cent post graduates, 69 per cent have retired from services, while 31 per cent are simply housewives, for 93 per cent their spouses are alive and for 7 per cent their spouses have expired, 80 per cent have the privilege of living with the family, 12 per cent lead their life alone and 8 per cent are unfortunate to live in the old age homes, and 80 per cent have no dependents while 20 per cent have dependents at the maximum of 3 members.

Table 12.5 : Problems of Old Age

Variables	Number	%
1	2	3
Difficulty in Concentrating	10	40
Sad and/or Crying	11	44
Angry	8	32
Overeating	10	40
Less Eating	5	20
Increased Amounts of Sleep	8	32
Decreased Amounts of Sleep	6	24
Irritable	6	24
Worried	8	32
Anxious	8	32
Indecisive	8	32
No Energy/Lethargic	10	40
Physical Aches or Pains	14	56
Misusing Alcohol, Tobacco or Other Drugs	8	32
Compulsive Thoughts	10	40
Feeling of insecurity	11	44
Racing Thoughts	12	48
Argumentative/Fighting	10	40
Communication Issues	3	12
Guilty	5	20
Hopeless	5	20
Worthless	5	20

1	2	3
Overwhelmed	6	24
Alone	6	24
Isolated	6	24
Feeling like No One Understands	11	44
Loss of Appetite	11	44
Lazy	10	40
No Motivation	12	48
Feeling as Though You Don't Care About Anything	7	28
Thoughts of Death, Suicide or Harming Someone	6	24
Pessimistic/Negative Outlook	8	32

Source: Primary Survey.

Physical Aches or Pains (56%), Racing Thoughts (48%), No Motivation (48%), Sad and Crying (44%), Feeling of insecurity (44%), Loss of Appetite (44%), and Feeling like No One Understands (44%) are the major problems encountered by the elderly in their course of life. Difficulty in Concentrating, Overeating, No Energy, Compulsive Thoughts, Argumentative/Fighting, and Laziness each having 40 percent are the other types of problems faced by the elderly. Other problems mentioned in the list are minor as per the opinion of the sample respondents.

Table 12.6 : Levels of old age problems

Levels of old age problems	No of respondents	%
Low level	231	87
Medium level	20	8
High level	13	5
Total	**264**	**100**

Source: Primary Survey.

The opinions on the old age problems are gathered from the sample respondents on a five point scale. The points on 0 and 1 are considered as low levels, 2 and 3 are medium levels and 4 and 5 are high levels. The analysis shows that 88 percent fall under low level of problems, 8 percent under medium level and 5 percent under high level. The same is depicted through Fig. 12.2 as below.

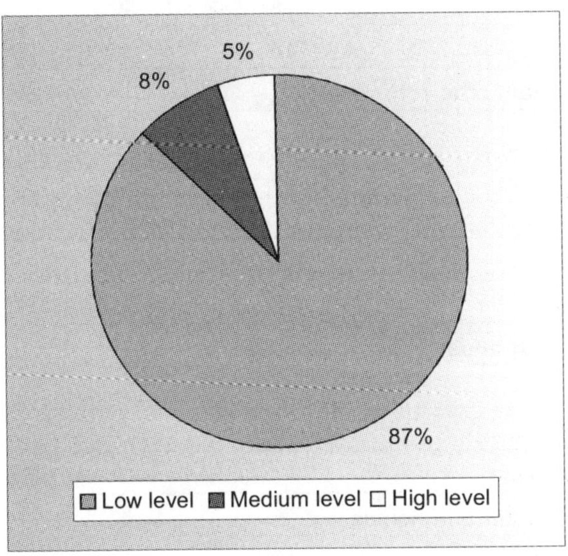

Fig. 12.2. Levels of Old age Problems

Table 12.7 : Levels of old age problems

Variables	Levels		
	Low	Medium and high	Total
1	2	3	4
Age			
Below 70	11	2	13
Above 70	11	1	12

1	2	3	4
Education			
School	12	1	13
Degree	10	2	12
Sex			
Male	8	2	10
Female	14	1	15
Employment after retirement			
Yes	1	1	2
No	21	2	23
Occupation			
Retired	16	1	17
Housewives	6	2	8
Status of Spouse			
Living	22	1	23
Expired	0	2	2
Mode of living			
Single and old age homes	6	2	8
Family Dependents	16	1	17
Nil	17	1	18
1-3	5	2	7
Nature of employment			
Government	11	0	11
Non-Government	11	3	14
Income			
Below 10000	17	2	19
Above 10000	5	1	6
Total	**22**	**3**	**25**

Source: Primary Survey

The levels of old age problems are measured through Yule's Coefficient of association. For this purpose, the variables are fitted in a two into two tabular forms. The personal variables and economic variables are compared with the levels of old age problems.

Table 12.8 : Yule's Coefficient of Association

Variables	Association
Age	-.33
Sex	-.63
Education	.41
Employment after retirement	-0.83
Occupation	.68
Status of Spouse	1
Mode of living	-0.68
Dependents	0.74
Nature of employment	1
Income	0.37

Source: Primary Survey.

Perfect association prevails between the levels of old age problems and the status of spouse and Nature of employment. Usually the old age problems are less when the couples live together, but the problem is acute when they are departed. In the same way permanent employment gives regular returns and those who worked in the private concerns do face with the problems in the old age. The association is negative in case of age, sex, Employment after retirement, and Mode of living and so these variables have no influence over the old age problems, but the sample respondents do suffer with the problems of looking after the Dependents. Further the variables like Occupation, Education, and Income do have influence over the level of old age problems.

Financial Abuse: Financial Abuse is another name for stealing or defrauding someone of goods and/or property.

It is always a crime but is not always prosecuted. Sometime the issue is straightforward, for example a care worker stealing from an older person's purse, but at other times it is more difficult to address. This is because very often the perpetrator can be someone's son or daughter, or age prejudice means that other people assume it is not happening or that the older person is to blame.

Table 12.9 : Financial Abuse

Particulars	Yes	No	%
1	2	3	4
Taking money or property	11	14	44
Forging the signature	4	21	16
Getting an older person to sign a deed, will, or power of attorney	1	24	4
Using the older person's property or possessions without permission	6	19	24
Promising lifelong care in exchange for money or property and not following through on the promise	5	20	20
Confidence crimes	3	2	12
Scams or fraudulent or deceptive acts	1	24	4
Dishonest acts or statements for financial gain	7	18	28
Use of credit cards without authorization	2	23	8
Sudden changes in Bank account or Banking practice	4	21	16
Unexplained withdrawal of large sums of money	2	23	8

1	2	3	4
Inclusion of additional names on an elder's bank signature card	3	22	12
Unauthorized withdrawal of the elder's funds using the elder's ATM card	5	20	20
Abrupt changes in a will or other financial documents	4	21	16
Unexplained disappearance of funds or valuable possessions	2	23	8
Substandard care being provided or bills unpaid despite the availability of adequate financial resources	6	19	24
Discovery of an elder's signature being forged for financial transactions or for the titles of his/her possessions	1	24	4
Sudden appearance of previously uninvolved relatives claiming their rights to an elder's affairs and possessions	2	23	8
Unexplained sudden transfer of assets to a family member or someone outside the family	2	23	
An elder's report of financial exploitation	1	24	4
Personal belongings such as jewellery, art, furs are missing	2	23	8
Cheatings by Care takers	4	21	16

Source: Primary Survey

The mean score is 3.55 and the standard deviation is 3.32. The levels are calculated by taking into account the two parameters. The high levels are obtained by adding standard deviation with mean, low levels are calculated by deducting the standard deviation from mean and the medium levels are calculated by considering the values lies between the higher level and lower level. Here the score 7 and above is considered as high level, 1 to 7 is considered as medium level, and below 1 is considered as low level. There are 92 percent of the sample respondents have medium level of financial abuse while 8 percent have medium level of financial abuse and nobody has low level of financial abuse. As most of the elder people in the study area are well aware of the financial abuses after retirement, well planning in advance save them a lot from the financial abuses.

Conclusion

The field of elder abuse prevention is multidisciplinary by nature. Professionals ranging from physicians to police officers are likely to encounter abuse cases and are in key positions to offer help. It is only recently that the attention of the world community has been drawn to the social, economic and political issues related to this phenomenon of ageing on a massive scale. As the world's population ages and the traditional role of the family as the main support of older people weakens, the elderly are increasingly vulnerable to abuse and various forms of negative stereotyping and discrimination. They often have limited access to health care and face specific age-related restrictions in many fields, such as job discrimination in hiring, promotion and dismissal. Furthermore, as many industrialised countries struggle with the task of adapting their social and economic policies to the ageing of their populations, even in affluent societies many older persons live in conditions of poverty. In developing countries with limited social security systems, the emigration of the younger members has left the elderly, traditionally cared for by members of their families, to fend for themselves. The survey reveals that though the sample respondents do vary in various respects, they face old age problems and financial abuses mildly. Careful planning and execution of secured savings and settlements will help the elders from attempting various forms of abuses. It is in the hands of the Government and Nongovernmental organisations to lend a supporting hand and to lift them up from the abuses in life.

Recommendations: The following recommendations are put forward based on the study results.

Depression: Depression can be an issue for older adults much as it can be for individuals of any age. Contrary to common myth, depression is highly treatable in old age. Rapid intervention and treatment is particularly essential as there is a high risk of suicide for elders. The methods like recreation, relaxation, participation and the like will keep their mind young and chase away the attitude of depression in the old age.

Isolation: There is a clear cut correlation between social support and life satisfaction. As life satisfaction decreases the risk for self-neglect increases. Isolation is a risk factor for all forms of elder abuse. Intervention entails the creation of trust, increased involvement of the older adult in the community, and the creation of social supports. This, of course, may be problematic for those individuals who have had little social support throughout their life-span. This situation can be eradicated by creating a network among the isolated elders.

Maintain social contacts: Increasing network of friends, keeping in touch with old friends and neighbours, developing a buddy system with a friend outside the home, and Participating in social and community activities will help the elder persons to get rid of the abuses in life. Further, involvement in the social services activities will help the elders to keep their mind busy and easy.

Awareness: Public awareness and professional training in relation to elder abuse and other older adult issues, assertiveness training, promotion of elder rights, and self-advocacy training for all older adults, adequate caregiver training and services will help the elder to get in touch with the society in a meaningful way.

Counselling: Counselling for victims or vulnerable adults can help them assess their options, plan for their safety, resolve conflicts, and overcome trauma. Educating victims about resources and options, breaking through denial and shame, safety planning, and building support networks can be done through counselling. Further Family counselling help to resolve or mediate conflicts and address tensions or stresses that give rise to abuse or neglect among elderly people.

Legal assistance: Legal assistance is needed in many abuse cases. Legal services are provided by private attorneys, programs operated by local or state bar associations, or subsidized legal aid programs. Lawsuits to recover assets or property, restraining orders to restrict contact between perpetrators and victims, prosecution of offenders, arranging guardianship and giving assistance to obtain restitution are the legal ways through which the elders can find shelter legally from the various abuses which often threatens them.

Money management: Financial abuse frequently may occur when an older person has lost the ability to manage his or her finances. Arranging for trustworthy people to help can reduce this risk. The help may be informal, where the money manager simply helps the elder with simple tasks like paying bills, or it may involve formal transfers of authority, including representative payee ship, power of attorney, or guardianship. This will be a booster to the elderly in getting rid of the financial abuses which they commonly encounter.

REFERENCES

Arthur Van Soest, 2006. *'Savings, Portfolio Choice, and Retirement Expectations'* Michigan Retirement Research Centre, University of Michigan.

Axel Borsch and Supan, 2004. *'Global Ageing; Issues, Answers, More Questions'* Michigan Retirement Research Centre, University of Michigan

Barry. P. Bosworth, 2004. *'The Impact of Aging on Financial Markets and the Economy: A Survey'*, Centre for Retirement Research at Boston College.

Gupta, S.P. Statistical Methods, S. Chand & Co., New Delhi, 2000.

Richard I. Levin and David S. Rubin, *Statistics Management*, Prentice-Hall India, 2002.

www.indiabudget.ac.in

Psycho-emotional Problems of the Aged Women at Care Homes

— Anbu Selvi

ABSTRACT

Old age is the last or later period in the life span. Like every other period in the human life span old age is characterized by certain physical and psychological changes. In this period people suffer from a lot of problems mainly psychological in nature. When the families are not able to manage the elders at homes due to one or other reasons they are taken care of in the home for the aged. This qualitative study examines the nature of psycho-emotional problems faced by the elderly women and the interpersonal relationship issues in a care-home in Coimbatore district of Tamil Nadu. It is expected that the research findings would greatly benefit social work educators and students; NGOs and SHG would become better sensitive to the problem faced by elderly in the care-homes; also, specific counselling services could be planned for the elderly residing in the care-homes.

Introduction

Aging as a social problem is relatively new in the Indian scenario. After the advancement of modern medicines and disease control all over the world the population of elderly has increased significantly and the problem of the aged increased. Life expectancy in India has increased by nearly 50 percent since 1960, says India Health Report 2010 (Confederation of Indian Industry (CII) and Indicus Analytics). India now has the second largest aged population in the world.

The elderly are a precious asset for any country. With rich experience and wisdom, they contribute their might for sustenance and progress of the nation. Today one can say that in India old age is a period of neglect and suffering. Their special health and economic issues differ from those of the general population. The United Nations Principles address the independence, participation, care, self-fulfilment and dignity of older persons as an ensured priority.

Old age period in human life is characterized by major physical and psychological changes. There is no consensus among scientist in defining the old age chronologically. Some authors define it above 50 years of age and some studies identify as 55, while other studies show 60 and above. Psycho-social problems could be defined as the psychological and sociological problems faced by someone, where in psycho means something related to mind and socio means something related to the society.

Majority of the problems that confront elderly people are social isolation and apparent reduction in family support, poverty and financial constraints, impairment of physical as well as cognitive functioning, mental illness, widowhood, limited options for living arrangement and dependency towards end of life. All these problems have an impact on the quality of life in old age and health care. In the traditional Indian societies, joint family system used to take care of most of these social issues. However, with industrialization and urbanization, disintegration of traditional joint family has caused havoc in the life of elders. Many social scientists argue that it is necessary to strengthen the traditional family system through community education and social intervention to safeguard the elders in the Indian society.

The aim of the study was to identify conflicts, stress, and strain and, adjustment issues of the elderly women in a selected home for the aged run by some missionary social workers.

Methodology

This study was conducted in an aged home near Coimbatore. This study used focused group discussion to obtain information from all the aged women inmates. From the focus group discussion, themes and categories were derived. A theoretical editing analysis protocol was used to develop conceptual theme by identifying meaningful segments, categories and provisional themes.

Results and Discussion

This study contradicts a major common belief that India is a land where age and wisdom are respected. The study results depict the fact that the society is moving from traditional values to Western values. The overall trend in the Indian communities, both rural as well as urban, is a rapid change in values regarding family and people in which elders are rejected by family members, neighbours and even they are denied rental houses.

The major conflicts and stressors of the people studied would be classified in to following categories: Feeling of isolation and alienation from families; loneliness and despair in some cases and the overall feeling of neglect. However, the study results identify a positive attitude in the life of the elders in the institutionalised care home. They are well-adjusted to the care-home conditions and feel more secure and have less suicidal tendencies. This also tells the fact that if proper care and concerns given, elderly people can feel at home in any place.

A general feeling of alienation is commonly seen among all the inmates. It could be identified as 'empty-nest syndrome' and the intensity of this feeling varies from individual to individual and largely depends upon the general personality make up of the individual. This study also confirms with the previous studies done in other parts of the world that an individual responsiveness towards alienation ranges from mild to severe. The majority of the inmates felt that "nothing much one could do about it" and have accepted as the inevitable fact of life, while a few are still struggling to cope with this syndrome with a greater feeling of loneliness, grief and sadness.

Lieberman (1996) has identified (in a study done in western society) that institutionalized elderly people have in common poor adjustment, depression, unhappier, intellectual ineffectiveness and poor in social participation. However, the current study in the Indian scenario contradicts this view and only a few members isolate themselves whereas majority of the inmates take part in every activity that took place in the home.

As for the feeling of insecurity the study subjects feel secure in the aged home as compared to the people outside. It is because they are getting good psychological support from the institution where they are staying. However few members of the group felt otherwise.

Suicidal tendencies and the fear of death are not seen among the inmates. They popularly believe that 'No one has the right to commit suicide, and life is a God given entity and He alone can take it away'. When probed the reason for this positive thought, all the members acknowledged that the effect of regular and spiritual programme given to them in the institution and the personal involvement of the care givers have resulted in this positive outlook on life and death.

Conclusion

Institutionalization is a worldwide phenomenon for the aged and elderly and it is becoming popular today in the Indian subcontinent. Aged people are institutionalized due to various reasons: lack of care givers at home; adjustment issues with family people and family burdens; deserted by family members; daughter-in-law issues; poor economic conditions. Once institutionalised, the elderly people need various adjustments, generally effective adaptation to the new environment. This adaptation is not easy in the old age because elders need to change their mental setup to live in a place away from home, with strangers and with less individual freedom abiding to the rules and regulations of the centre. Good adjustments expand itself in happiness, confidence, contentment, sociability, freedom and morbid emotion.

From the study the causes identified that create adjustment problems are feeling of isolation and alienation from families, loneliness and despair in some cases and the overall feeling of neglect from family members. The study also identifies that when proper love and care is given, elderly people can cope with their old age related issues even in the care homes. The findings also points out regular spiritual programme are very beneficial for the elders. When such spiritual programmes are given within the institution together with the personal involvement and commitment of the care givers, positive attitudes are seen among the institutionalised elderly people.

Recommendations

(1) Appointment of social workers in the institution is recommended for giving regular motivational and occupational programmes.

(2) The availability of periodic medical check-up keep the inmate freer from health related problems.

(3) A warm relationship between the inmates and the care-givers can create positive attitude among the elderly.

(4) Making the elderly inmates participate in spiritual and recreational activities regularly will revive their desire to live and die happily.

(5) Institutional caregivers should be trained in counselling skills and conducting psycho-spiritual programmes so that the elders can be motivated for happy and peaceful living.

REFERENCES

Elizabeth.B.Hwlock (1981). *Developmental psychology, a life span approach*, Tata McGraw-Hill.

Gordon, S.K. (1973). Phenomenon of depression in old age, *The Gerontologist (1973) 13(1): 100-105.*

Liptzin, B., & Salzman, C. (1988). Psychiatric aspects of aging. In J. W. Rowe and R. W. Besdine (Eds.), *Geriatric Medicine*, (pp. 355-374). Boston: Little Brown.

Mace, N.L.(1989). Special Care Units for Dementia Patients, *Provider,* pp. 10-12.May.

A Comparative Study on the Life of Elders and Related Abuses at Families and Care Centres

— R. Renukadevi,
— E. Saradha

ABSTRACT

The elderly people are respected in our Indian society, because they are the guardian of moral and traditional Indian values in the families in particular and society in general. But, nowadays they are assaulted and neglected due to misunderstanding between the inmates of their own houses and neighbourhoods. Due to the change from joint family system to nuclear ones, urban migrations in search of better living conditions, increased number of family people looking for jobs outside the families and migration from native villages to nearby towns and cities, taking care of elders in the families become a problem. The net result is that elderly people are forced to be in care centres. This leads to the increased old age homes in our country. In the old age homes also elders face problems and lead a life of troubles. The loneliness of the elderly people in the care centre leads to stress and desolation. This research is a comparative analysis of the condition of elder people in the families and care centres.

This qualitative study was conducted at two different places in Tamil Nadu namely Trichy and Udumalpet. In-depth unstructured interview with some guide questions, two researchers collected data from families and care centres in the months of May and June 2010. The data collected was categorized into themes to identify similarities and differences in the treatment old people get in both the places as well as the overall feelings of elderly people in both the places.

The study results provide a clear sketch of elderly abuse in both the places. This study will further lead to minimize the misunderstanding between young and elderly people in houses as well as care centres. The study brings to limelight the changing traditional values and the modern society and its impact on elderly people.

Introduction

The elderly people are respected in our Indian society, because they are the guardian of moral and traditional values in the families in particular and society in general. But, nowadays they are assaulted and neglected due to various reasons. The change from joint family system to nuclear ones, urban migration in search of better living conditions increase the number of family people looking for jobs outside their native villages and birth places leading to increased incidents of parental neglect. Conditioned by this socio-economic scenario, taking care of elders in the families becomes a problem for many especially couples who are employed. The ultimate result is that elderly people are forced to be in care centres. This leads to the increased number of old age care homes in our country. As the number of care-homes increase, concern over the abuses against elder people comes to limelight. It is generally accepted that elder people are unable, frightened or embarrassed to face as well as report the abuses.

The problems of elder people have become a social problem in our society. The changes in the demographic structure during the last few decades have made the elderly people's status a more noticeable section in the society. The changing of family structure in the recent decades accelerated the problem of elderly people in the families. Due to economical constraints and irresolvable misunderstanding with younger generation, the elderly people are forced to take shelter in the care centres. In care centres too, elder people face a lot of problems. So, they hate to survive in care centres too.

This study is mainly focused on the present conditions of elderly people in the families and care canters. Due to misunderstanding of youth in families or due to various other reasons, the elderly people are forced to be in the care centres. When elders face problems in the families, they are forced to go to care-homes. Are they comfortable and safe in the care-homes? In care homes too, they face lot of problems with the caregivers and other inmates in the homes. The study aims at comparing the situation in both the places.

Methodology

This qualitative study was conducted at Trichy and Udumalpet towns in Tamil Nadu. An unstructured interview was conducted to understand the feeling and problems of elderly people. Data collection was done in the months of May-June 2010 by two researchers. The study results provide a clear outline of elderly abuse in both the places. 20 elderly people were interviewed in the care centre and 30 were interviewed living in the families. Collected data were categorized into themes. The study results will pave way for more understanding among young and elderly people both in house as well as care centres to minimize the misunderstanding and issues related to that. It will create awareness about the traditional value and the modern changing society and its impact on the people.

Evolved Themes and Categories

Abuses in the Families	Abuses in the Care-homes
1. Not allowed to go to relatives homes, confined to family home	Care is given only for namesake
2. Children do not want us and we are a burden feeling	Rarely family members visit and feeling of loneliness
3. Used as domestic servants at home without rest	Elders are forced to do given work by the supervisor
4. Pension money is taken by the family members and every expenditure is questioned	Caregivers cheat us in money matters
5. Shouting and yelling (verbal abuse) by family members	Caregivers scold with hard words (verbal abuse)
6. Beaten up, kicked and physical objects thrown at them (physical abuse)	Kick and spank them (physical abuse)
7. Neglected, not respected	Loneliness

Case One: Mr X is 65 years old, staying in a care-centre narrated his main concern in the following way: He is suffering from spinal injury and poor eyesight. His main pain in the care-centre is spending time fruitfully. He feels that he is neglected by the family as well as people in the centre. His children justify that they have done their duty by paying his accommodation and related expenses. The people in the centre feel that they do their duty when they provide food and shelter. He still feels that there is more in life beyond food and money which he is not able to do or identify or fulfil. He also feels that the care-givers abuse him verbally.

Case Two: A diabetic patient, who is admitted in the centre because her children are migrated to the city due to job concerns. According to her, the caregivers do not give her regular attention and proper assistance whenever she approaches them. The caregivers are not assisting her to toilet at times. Often she was scolded by the caregivers for dirtying the bed and the surrounding places. Her problem as well as the related verbal abuse from the warden put her in a pathetic situation.

Case Three: An elderly woman of 70 years laments that the pocket-money that was given by her son was taken by the person in-charge of the old home. This has become a regular occurrence and she is not able to complain to anyone. Whenever she complaints the wardens shout at her telling that she has amnesia or telling lies. She does not know how to overcome from this financial abuse.

Case Four: This is a tale of an old widow, who was forced to be in a care centre due to the unbearable torture from her daughter-in-law. According to her, the son has become a hen-pecked husband and not able to control his wife. She even suspects that the daughter-in-law and her family people might have done some witchcraft and sort of things to change the mind of her son. She was regularly assaulted at home and showed in her hands bruises and marks of being beaten by her own family members. This made her to come to the care centre somewhat voluntarily. Once she came here her son never came to visit her. At the care-centre also she is not at peace. She is over burdened with works of different nature. She is forced to do physical labour.

Case Five: This is a story of an elderly lady who is working as a domestic servant. She could earn hardly few rupees daily. Her son is an alcohol addict and treats her brutally in order to extract her poor earnings. She showed her swollen face slapped by her son demanding money to drink alcohol. Although her neighbours requested her to file a case in the nearby police station, she refused to do that because it is his son and doesn't want to jeopardise his future. This good will of the mother is exploited by the drunkard son.

Case Six: A retired school teacher narrated his account of torture and abuse in the family in the following way. His problems in the family originate from the irresponsible son and the hard-hearted daughter-in-law. His pension money is taken forcibly by his son. The extra income he gets from tuition for small children is also taken by his son and daughter-in-law. He is kept alive at home because the son is waiting to grab the property once he dies. The son does not even think that this elder person is his father and abuses him to the maximum. This elderly person is mentally depressed with all kinds of abuses he faces at home.

Conclusion

The study has identified nearly 80% of the elderly people face problems and abuses in one of another form. In some cases it is the family that abuses the elders, sometimes they are abused in the centres where they shelter for their problems and still some elders are abused at both family as well as the centres. Even though there are many campaigns to safeguard the elders, like World Elder Abuse Awareness Day (WEAAD), National Adult Day Services Association (NADSA), Adult Day Health Care" (ADHC), and many more, the elders are in precarious situation. The Indian government has also drafted regulations to punish the children when they neglect their duties towards their parents. However the problem in India still remains a threat to the core values and traditions of our country.

The Spaces of Elderly People in Urban Delhi

— Dr. Nawal P. Singh

ABSTRACT

Elderly people are having various spaces in thought, family, society and resources. There are obvious individual differences based on the activities and economic resources. This study describes the current scenario of elderly people in the Indian capital Delhi. The study used qualitative techniques of participant observation and disguised observation as the primary sources of data from public places and casual conversation at parks, temples and shopping malls and market places.

The study identifies three categories of elders in the urban Delhi. The first category is the retired employees from middle class and lower middle class who have minimal source of income from their pension money, have some or a little space in family and society. Due to nature of traditional rural joint family system and the growing tendency for nuclear family, they are often considered a pest in the family, partially neglected and left out and branded as a burden.

The second category of elders is the business class. This category often looks after traditional family businesses with a regular source of income and they are in a better position than the previous category with sustainable space in family and society. However, they too have their own share of pain and agony in the old age. Apparently they have lesser worry and pain. The third group of elders who are people in the lowest stratum, who were neither government employees nor sustainable business people, are the target by the family members in a maximum abusive manner and often assigned the daily chores of house like buying vegetables, milk, bread and butter in morning and evening with a treatment not better than a housemaid or house worker.

The study brings out the abusive and painful life of old age and the need for social reform, better understanding from the part of youngsters and more stringent laws to safeguard the rights of elders in India.

Introduction

Elderly people are having various spaces in thought, family, society and resources. There are obvious individual differences based on the activities and economic resources. This study describes the current scenario of elderly people in the Indian capital Delhi. The study used qualitative techniques of participant observation and disguised observation as the primary source of data at public places and casual conversation at parks, temples and shopping places.

Delhi is the second largest metropolis in India with a population of above 22.5 million population. This is the eighth largest in the world. It is on the banks of Yamuna river, Inhabited from 6th Century BCE. Today, it stands as the major cultural, political, and commercial centre of India. One could see today both the old (Chandni Chowk) as well as the new (Chanakyapuri). Ultramodern posh bungalows and richest people at the one side of the city at the same time shanties and ghettos on the other side.

Although it is the National Capital city, it has its own problems for the people who reside in Delhi. The day-to-day problems that affect the people of Delhi could be viewed from three major angles as identified by an unknown blogger. (*i*) *Corruption* - there has been a lot of corruption in Delhi since many years, in every area of life. Contaminated and adulterated food products are major concern for healthy living. We live with a corrupted political system that is reflected directly on the roads in the form of police officers, politicians, etc. ii) *Traffic* - due to the slow developmental works and the corruption associated with every government public work contract, all the road works are prolonged for months and months which could be normally finished within a week. This leads to constant traffic jam in every nook and corner of the streets causing air and noise pollution which affects the overall lifestyle of the people living there. In one street there is traffic jam due to the small size of the road and in another place there is traffic jam due to expansion works on the road. (*iii*) *Poverty* - The increased urban migration and the ever changing economic situation leads to increased number of poor people in the city try to shelter creating their own slums and ghettos all over empty spaces as well as sidewalks. One can spot poor people even at sewage dumps looking for tiny objects and materials for their living, and begging at road junctions. If this is the case on the outside, the situation at home or families also have their own turmoil.

The urban Delhi families are not different than the rural Indian families. The problems we see and hear in the rural communities are also prevalent in the urban communities in different forms. This study is mainly focused on the space the elders experience and have at their families.

Methodology

This is a qualitative research with participant observation and disguised observation as the primary sources of data. Besides these, interview of 245 people in the form of casual conversation at parks, temples and shopping malls and market places were used to collect data for further analysis.

Results and Discussion

The study identifies three categories of elders in the urban centre.

Table 15.1 : Retired Employees from Middle class and lower middle class

Space	In Relation
Moderate	Son
Low	Daughter in-law
Moderate	Daughter
Moderate	Grandson/Daughter
Low	Among relatives

Identified Causes:

1. Traditional habits and views
2. I am always right attitude
3. I like to have everything in my own way situation
4. Employment behaviors not forgotten and taunting
5. Economic implications and related life conditions

Table 15.2 : Elderly Business Class

Space	In Relation
Moderate	Daughter in-law
Moderate	Daughter
Moderate	Grandson/Daughter
Moderate	Among relative

Identified Causes:

1. Son is dependent on father business and the feeling of safety
2. An elderly person is always behind the son business giving physical and moral support
3. More adjustability because of business cooperation under compulsion

Table 15.3 : Elderly people in lower strata

Space	In Relation
Low	Son
Low	Daughter in-law
Moderate	Daughter
Low	Grandson/Daughter
Moderate	Among relative

Identified Causes:

1. Least finance support for elders
2. Elders are a burden in the family
3. Daughters on sympathetic ground often unable to bear the burden
4. Younger generation are fond of English language and the widening gap

The first category is the retired employees from middle class and lower middle class who have minimal source of income from their pension money have some or a little space in family and society. Due to nature of traditional rural joint family system to the urban nuclear family, they are often considered a pest in the family, partially neglected and left out and branded as a burden. The second category of elders is the business class. This category often looks after traditional family businesses with a regular source of income are in a better position than the former with sustainable space in family and society. However, they too have their own share of pain and agony in the old age. Apparently they have lesser worry and pain. There is yet another group of elders who are people in the lowest stratum, who were neither government employees nor sustainable business people, become the target by the family members in a maximum abusive manner and often assigned the daily chores of house like buying vegetables, milk, bread and butter in morning and evening with a treatment not better than a house maid and house worker. They pass their free time in the temples, *gurudwaras*, parks and public places pondering over their glorious past, brooding on their pathetic present and also contemplate on their uncertain future.

In short we can pinpoint the elder abuse in the Metro Delhi in the following way.

1. Retired are either alone or backside in house or home
2. Business class having good space in house but interaction with grandchildren is low because of language
3. Lower income group are abandoned or backside in Home/house
4. In multi-storeyed building, elderly people are unable to see park or road because they need support to come down. Even some of the older people who are well but unable to come down due to lack of physical support.
5. Apparent and pronounced abuses in the family
6. Often elders become both the victim as well as the persecutor
7. Women are most abused

The elders in general are targeted and abused by every category of family members. Modern education and the globalization have made the gap between elders and other members in the family. The small children in the house can't converse with their grandparents who do not speak English. So the elders are not approached by the children in the houses. Adolescent children feel that there is a generation gap between the elders and themselves and see elders as a watchman who curtail their freedom and impose their old values and traditions. The adult children in the houses target only the money and the properties of the elders and this becomes life-threatening to the elders at times. Many elderly people have been killed by their relatives for properties in the urban capital.

In the public places too, they are the easy prey to the anti-socials in the parks, shopping complexes and public places, rob and stripe them off the little penny they have. Reckless drivers abuse them verbally and also kill them in accidents by mere negligence. In the public transports and shopping places they are abused and cheated.

Conclusion

The study has identified the inevitable outcome of this situation is the rise of aged homes in a society that is not prepared for this phenomenon. So the elders are in an unforgivable situation when the family members think of entrusting the elders in a care home. This abusive and painful life of old age and the need for social reform, better understanding from the part of youngsters and more stringent laws to safeguard the rights of elders in India. Based on the study results the following conclusions can be drawn and certain recommendations are suggested.

1. Economic status of the family and economical security are the defining factors of elder abuse in Urban Delhi.
2. Understanding the elders by the younger generation is highly recommended.
3. Regaining our traditional values - mainly respect for elders and tolerance is must to safeguard the elders
4. Besides economical security, good hobbies and friends network can help the elders to manage boredom and loneliness

The Condition of Elderly People at Social Places

A Study at Three Bus Stations

– B. Sutharsan,
Ms. R. Sandhya

ABSTRACT

In the Indian society, traditionally the elderly people are respected and taken care of in many ways. Elderly people are considered as the backbone of society. Unfortunately, in our Indian society this scenario is changing. Elderly people in our society are sometimes viewed as nuisance and not valued the way they are respected traditionally. Seniors are verbally abused, neglected in their homes, in the society and in their workplaces. Social isolation leading to loneliness is also, a main concern today. This study aims at describing the current situation of elderly people in public places, specifically at bus stations. Secondly, it identifies whether any abuse takes place at the bus station and what kinds of abuses are prevented finally. Expectations of elderly people regarding their condition at bus stations are identified. This qualitative study was conducted in three bus stations namely Pollachi and Udmalaipettai in Tamilnadu and Kozhijamparai in kerala state. The methods used were disguised observation, participant observation and casual interaction with elderly people at the above mentioned bus stations. The data was collected by two researchers two hours per day randomly for a period of 10 days. The study brings out a clear picture of abuse of elders in public places. Further the study will create awareness among the elders to expect and mange such situations. The study also will in a minimal way reduce human right abuse by making the aware public of each situation.

Introduction

The ageing process is of course a biological reality which has its own dynamism, largely beyond human control. However, it is also subject to the constructions by which each society makes sense of old age. In developed world, chronological time plays a paramount sole. The age of 60 or 65, roughly equivalent to retirement ages in most developed countries is said to be the beginning of old age. In many parts of the developing world, chronological time has little or no importance in the meaning old age.

Other socially constructed meanings of age are more significant such as the roles assigned to older people, in some cases it is the loss of roles accompanying physical decline which is significant in defining old age. Thus, in contrast to the chronological milestones which mark life stages in the developed world, old age in many developing countries is seen to begin at the point when active contribution is no longer possible (Gorman).

Traditionally elder care has been the responsibilities of families as well as society members. But increasingly in modern societies, abuses are taking place more and more in societies and homes instead of providing care. Although these changes have affected European and North American countries, it is now increasingly affecting India also. In our country the people are following traditional culture and the respect for elders is more, which won't make harm to elderly and therefore abuses are less especially in public places when compared to homes.

According to the "National Committee for the Prevention

of Elder Abuse" in America "Professionals in the field of aging are often the first to discover the signs of elder abuse", therefore most countries have established laws that define elder abuse and require care provide to report any cases they encounter with penalties attached for failing to do so. In India, not much laws are there to safeguard elders; also no media attention has been focused on elderly abuse that takes place in society.

This study evaluates the current situations of the elderly people in the social places especially in bus stations. Based on the reports of the elderly people and added suggestions from the officers working in bus stations, the authors propose some measures to help elderly people to clear up the abuses from the bus stations.

The objectives of the study:

1. Describing the current situation of elder people in bus stations.
2. To identify the kinds of abuses that takes place at the bus stations.
3. Expectations of elderly people regarding their conditions at bus stations.

Methodology

This is a qualitative study that describes the scenario of elderly people at public places. The authors used the methods of disguised observation, participant observation and causal interaction with elderly people at the bus stations to collect data. The main focus of casual interactions was to know "the expectations of elders at bus stations". Data were collected through and some causal interacts from 67 (passengers) elder peoples and 13 officers working in 3 bus stations at Pollachi, Udmalaipettai in the State of Tamil Nadu and Kozhijamparai in Kerala State.

The authors themselves observed the elders in three bus stations from 3rd - 9th of May 2010 and 24th - 25th of June 2010,

2 hours per day – randomly. Disguised observation, participant observation and casual interaction were used to collect data. Cooperation of the elder peoples and officers, differences of opinions were given high priority in collecting data.

The data from disguised observation, participant observation and causal interactions provided enough material for data analysis. As per the norms of qualitative study, themes and categories were derived from the data.

Results and Discussion

The results revealed that the average number of passenger passes through the bus station is 69 per cent and out of that the percentage of elders is high when comparing to youngsters *i.e.,* it lies in the ratio of 48 : 21. Among the 48 per cent elders most of them are out passers. The researcher spent 2 days for causal interaction among elders and 2 days for interacting with the officers. And they found that still there occurs some abuses in the bus station like physical, emotional exploitations and abandonment etc.

Table 16.1 : Observed Abuses

Sl. No.	Types of abuse	No. of people affected	Abused by
1.	Verbal abuse	23%	Youngsters and conductor
2.	Sexual harassments	-	-
3.	Physical abuse	09%	Youngsters
4.	Robbery/stealing	04%	Antisocial
5.	Neglect	02%	Family members
	Total	38%	

There are many cases of abuses and neglect with the elderly in the bus station today. There is an estimated cases of 38 out of every 100 elder people per day observed. Out of every cases observed and estimated 23 are abused by physically or verbally. It is said that people that live with abuses generally die earlier then the elderly without abuse. Elderly abuse is all around us and big percentage of abuses takes place in the social places like bus stand. A lot of elderly persons traveling in buses suffer from this social evil.

Table 16.2 : Narrated Abuses

Sl.No.	Types of abuse	Abused by
1.	Verbal abuse	Younger people
2.	Sexual harassments	-
3.	Physical abuse	Younger people
4.	Robbery/stealing	Antisocial
5.	Neglect	Shop owners
6.	Lack of respect	Shop owners, conductors, younger people

The data from disguised observation reveal that 60% elders are abused due to impaired mobility. As adult lose the ability to walk, to climb up and board the bus, they become completely disabled. The problem can't be ignored because people above 65 years of age constitute the fastest growing segment of Indian population.

Practical Examples

(Case 1) An old woman, with her heavy luggage and a crutch, got down from a bus coming from Coimbatore. A little boy in a lightning speed came there to get into the bus, he forced that woman outside and she fell down from the bus and got a severe wound on her knees and forehead. No one helped that woman except another elder woman. And the conductor also mercilessly abused her verbally. The elder woman got emotional as well as physical abuse.

(Case 2) Tears dripped down from a old lady's face as she lamented about her missing suitcase in the busy Udmalaipettai bus station. "It had my children's birth certificates, my money and my important files" she softly cried. It was a Saturday evening. She searched here and there and finally went out from the bus station. There was nobody to console her or enquire her what, when and where she lost her belongings. Each and every elderly person in the bus station have their own problems and hesitate to talk openly due to fear of verbal abuse from others and also irresponsive behaviour of the officers.

Expectation of Elder People in Bus Station

(1) Elders are expecting that the government should have a project to reduce elder abuse. Retired police officers should be hired by the government to act as a liaison between the social service agencies and seniors.

(2) An elder abuse unit office should be established in every bus station to prevent elders from getting abused.

(3) In each and every bus station, facilities like rest room, separate ticket counter, guards etc. should be allotted by the government to help the elder peoples.

(4) The society is unaware of the value of elderly people. This is the main problem which leads to abuse. So the government should create on awareness program about the valued elderly people and to avoid abuse.

Duties and Responsibilities of the Elderly Abuse Unit

(1) To focus on protecting India's older citizens from fraud and exploitation, through public education, as well as investigation and prosecution of exploitation cases.

(2) To assist in the investigation with other law enforcement agencies in elderly abuse cases.

(3) To investigate cases referred by Police services and any other agencies. The case would be of a complex nature of Verbal, material and financial exploitation of the elderly abuse.

(4) To present case of material and financial exploitations of the elderly for prosecution.

(5) To train other law enforcement agencies in the state of tamilnadu on the identification of elderly abuse, first contact.

Some Advice to Elders

(1) For older adults self-care is important too, especially when their activity is limited by illness. Go outside with a companion and keep your mind active.

(2) Stay active in the community. Social isolation is strongly connected with elder abuse. So if you are an older adult, it is important to stay connected.

(3) Some older adults feel embarrassed, ashamed or fearful to report any form of elder abuse. Please remember that the state and local communities have professional who have trained to handle elder abuse issues. So don't be afraid to speak up openly and file case with polices.

What could be done: Instead of looking for assistance in public places they can have their own ways of managing situations people can be educated to be more considerate towards elders. An elder abuse unit could be created in public places to safe-guard the rights of elders.

If you believe that you (older person) are a victim of any exploitation /abuse or you suspect that someone you know is a victim of any exploitation / abuse, you should contact the elder abusing unit / law enforcement agencies / adult protective service institution immediately without any fear or hesitation to report against the person who is making abuses.

Conclusion

The heart of an older person sometimes sinks with the sound of the word in social places, especially bus station, because these places have become the most common place for abuses. According to Erik Erikson's eight stages of life theory, the human personality is developed in a series of eight stages that takes place from the time of birth and continue on throughout an individual's complete life. He characterizes elder people are having the period of integrity Vs despair during which a person focuses on reflecting back on their life. So, we must make them proud at the end of their lifetime. It will only happen by fulfilling the elder people's expectations in the bus stations. If the expectations are not fulfilled the elder people will be left with feeling of bitterness and despair. It is only in the hands of younger generations because they are the future power of our country.

So, the study results will have the way for getting a clear picture of the human rights abuse on elders in public places, specifically in the bus stations. Further it will create awareness among the elders to expect and mange such situations. The study also will in a minimal way reduce human abuse by making the public aware to of such situations. We feel those data will pave way for adopting measures and promoting programmes. The accumulated evidence and resulting information will be able to help more accurately to determine the status of elder passengers in bus stations.

Changing Society and the Elderly People

Identifying Reasons for Mushrooming Aged Homes in India

— Arulappan

ABSTRACT

The study focuses on the issue of modernization and the elders as victims. The technological development led to Modernization. The modernization is the cause for urbanization and the urbanization is the cause for the migration in the society. Hence the migration from rural to urban has become unavoidable in India too. India is known for its traditional joint family system but there is a rapid change in this family scenario. As a result, the cultural transformation to nuclear family system is inevitable. Indian is forced to change to the new situation but there is cultural transition. Indians have failed to cope to its rapid modernization. The equilibrium between modernization and culture transition is not maintained. But the westerners have got accustomed to nuclear family. Their prime aim is individual freedom and privacy. But Indian are neither economically not emotionally independent. So elders of our country fail to digest the alienation from their children.

Through the interview methodology, the research tries to bring forth the existential problems are faced by the elderly people of middle class. It also helps to disclose the family and social discrimination of elderly men and women.

The economic independency could be one of the remedy to the problem of alienation but the emotional alienation will be a problem for long time unless the elders accept their fellow friends as emotional thirst means for emotional quenching.

Introduction

The changes are always unavoidable in the society. It is the change which brought human beings from the ancient to the industrialised society. We have moved from the stone-age, to the agricultural and today to the IT society. It is the change that makes life comfortable. Take for example our daily travel: one can easily reach Pollachi from Delhi in few hours of travel where as one needs to travel for at least a couple of days or even weeks few decades ago. Therefore, it is the needs and necessities of the human beings that initiated the advent of industrial revolution and the inevitable changes we see today. Everything has its own positive and negative effects. Likewise, the industrial revolution influenced the society and left its own impact on the society. The advent of industrialised civilization and the advancement of technology have not only caused tremendous changes in the society but also the stress and adjustment difficulties and above all the devastating changes in the traditional family values systems.

The introduction of industrial revolution made tremendous change in the society, especially in the family setup. For instance, in the olden days, when our ancestors worked in the field, both husband and wife together went to the field and returned back. A mutual reciprocal understanding prevailed in the family. This could be one of the reasons to have more number of children and a joint family system that gave support and assistance. The present social scenario is entirely different. In the present IT times, both husband and wife are working and they are earning more than what they expect for their family. At the same time they do not need the help of others. Therefore, they prefer the nuclear family system.

However, the negative impact of industrial and urban way of life has resulted in the inauguration of old age care homes at every city. In the olden days, family is the centre of the economic activities. The family took care of the entire family. So, somebody would be there in the family to take care of both the children and elderly people. But today, the size of the family and the economic security has almost vanished. Today, most of the people are feeling that large family is an economic liability instead of an economic asset. Consequently, they are preferring nuclear family. The breaking up of the old form of family system leads to high rate of child crimes and mushrooming of the aged homes.

Another important effect of the industrial revolution is mobility. As stated earlier, the family size decreased due to industrialised social setup. The modern family consists of parents and one or two children. After finishing their study, children have to go for job. When the children get employment opportunity away from their native place the children prefer to go but the parents don't like it. That means, when the children are ready to move from one place to another the parents are not ready due to various reasons.

In the modern society, sometimes the husband and wife have to live separately due to their profession and work situations. Under such a state of an affair, the wife will have to take care of her children alone. Consequently, she would not like to take her parents or in-laws. So, they prefer to send the elders into aged homes.

The industrial revolution has pushed the society in to a materialistic outlook. In the olden days the family members were bonded by love and affection. But, today, the family is purely materialistic. The earning members are not in a position to think of love and affection. Rather, they are fixated with earning more money and look for more economical security. Hence they are thinking twice to contribute something for their aged family members. The material culture made the father to stay away from the family. Consequently, leading to have lesser emotional attachment with his children giving the impression that father is money making machine. The father gets respect from the family members as long as he works and earns. Once he retires from job, he also automatically gets voluntary retirement from getting respect from family members.

Another change caused by the industrial revolution is the changes in the position of women. It is a good move in the society to see women come up many professional spheres. But its impact in the society is remarkable. Some opinion that since the lady is earning she doesn't have to depend on others and ultimately she is not interested to take care of her aging parents and in-laws. And also, when the lady is educated and the in-laws are not, it is difficult for the in-laws to adjust and to digest the lifestyle of their daughter in law.

In some cases, when differences appear among married couples, the wife likes to live separately with or without legal separation or divorce. It affects the growth of children psychologically, emotionally and socially. It leads the children to grow wanting in love and affection. Consequently, when these children mature, they fail to take care of their aging parents.

Objectives

Today, elderly people are facing lot of problems in the society. The study is aimed at identifying reasons for increasing aged homes in our country.

Methodology

Interview and case study methods were used to collect data. An informal negotiation method is used for collect information from aged people who are in care homes. The subjects of this study are 78 elders; 48 women and 30 men. Among them, two are couples, two Anglo-Indian people, two sisters from a same family, and a mother and her daughter.

Results and Discussion

The subjects of the study could be divided into two categories based on their economic status. They are: economically well group and middle class group. Out of 78 people, around 55 people belong to the rich people category and their children are in very good position. For example, one elder woman has two children. One is in USA and another child is a pilot. Then you can understand what their economic status is. In another case, the children sent the elder to the home after forcibly registered the land and property in his name. This shows that the children wants to enjoy their parents wealth but they do not like share their problems. The second group is poor group. Here, we can't blame the children. The children like to keep their parents with them. But, their economic condition does not allow them to take care. It is so, because, for the elderly people they have to provide medical facilities, healthy food and others. But, in the home all these will be provided in a better way. By hearing all these things, the children unwillingly bring their parents to the home.

Human rights are those rights that all human beings derive from the dignity and worth inherent in them. In a way "human rights are those minimal rights which every individual must have against the state or other public authority by virtue of his being a member of the human family, irrespective of any other consideration". Thus human rights are not dependent upon grant or permission. Rights and duties are complimentary to each other in a well-knit social fabric of any social organization. Rights are primarily intended to accord social justice to the human individuals. According to Philosopher Kant, a right has a power to create a sense of obligation or duty in an individual as a moral being. He further says that, "it is the restriction of each individual's freedom of everyone else". If X has a duty to leave Y alone or to provide him with some service, then Y has a right to that permission or service. It amounts to saying that rights necessarily involve social relations. Apart from that, a duty as an obligation is binding on individuals. Therefore, individuals are not praised for doing their duties. For instance, we do not praise a debtor for paying his debts. Here I like to say the children are like debtors.

In the olden days, people were not aware of human rights but were very much aware of their obligations towards their neighbours. Nowadays people are familiar with human rights but they conveniently forget human obligation. For example, today we talk about education as the right of children and the government and a number of NGOs are working for that. But we forget to incorporate in the children the value that they need to take care of their elderly parents. In the school itself we have to popularise these things. The parents are providing good education, food, cloth and everything even at the cost of sacrificing their needs.

Now, we have to approach this problem logically. Children enjoyed all the facility in the name of right. Similarly, parents provided all the facility in the name of duty/obligation. As stated earlier, every right have its own obligation. Likewise, the children enjoyed their childhood depending on their parents since it is their rights. Since they enjoyed their rights, they have to perform their obligation/duty. Their duty is to take care of their elderly parents. In other words, elderly people have the rights to depend on their children since they completed their duties in a good manner. We have to popularise the obligation of every children. Then elderly people problem will be solved.

As the results of the study identify, some parents are entrusted to care homes due to poverty. In this case, the parents accept the situation of their children and content with their life in the care-homes.

Today, we live with a more materialistic as well as pragmatic worldview. The negative aspect of the materialist world is that it gives importance to any physical comforts. At this social scenario we have to seed the idea of attachment and belongingness in the minds of youngsters. In some cases, the elderly parents do not like to adjust with their children. For example, in a family of one bedroom house, after the marriage the young couple prefer to sleep in the bed room. But the father will not be ready to give his bedroom to the married child. In this situation, the married people prefer to live alone and ultimately forgetting their obligations towards their elderly parents. So, we can solve many of the problems by means of mutual adjustments. That will be possible only when there is love and attachment among all the family members.

Finally, it will be easy to say that we can solve the elder's problem but, practically, it is very difficult. On the basis of the study results, apparently we may conclude that the children neglect their parents. At the same time, the other side of the problem would be the difficulty of the elderly people in adjusting to the needs of the other family members. Whether the children or the parents, wherever the problem lies, lack of attachment, commitment and adjustment increases the problem of human obligation.

REFERENCES

Basu, D. (1994). *Human rights in Constitutional Law*, New Delhi: Printince-Hall

Sehgal, B.P. (1999), *Human Rights in India: Problems and Perspectives*, New Delhi: Deep and Deep publications

Sharma, R.N. (1985). *Principles of Sociology*, Bombay: Media Promoters & Publishers

Singh, K. (1996). *Principles of Sociology*, Lucknow: Prakashan Kedra.

Stewart, W., Elbert & Glynn, J (1975). *A Introduction to Sociology*, New Delhi, Tata McGraw-Hill

Sundaresan, K. (1989). *Political philosophy of Immanuel Kant*, University of Madras.

CHAPTER

18

A Study on the Issues related to Taking Care of Elderly at Homes

— Shoby Bovas

ABSTRACT

Aging is a universal process and it affects each human being in the world. However the issues and problems related to aging differ from culture to culture. Today due to the technology and better medical care the process of aging has slowed down and the problems and issues related increase. Generally care taking means basic care given to a person who has a chronic medical condition. However managing elderly people at home too becomes care taking. It is because elderly people completely depended upon the family members for their daily needs. People who take care for elderly people at home are often stressed due to the strain of being attending the needs of the elderly. Taking care of elderly means we need to have all the responsibility of the mother of a little child, with none of the optimism and expectation because the person growing up will become dependent all the more as age grows. We may lose our sanity our financial wellbeing, physical health because taking care of elders drains us very much.

Taking care of elders is difficult, time consuming, emotionally and physically burdensome. Once the burdens become too great, and if the economical conditions of the family accept, families will forgo in favour of institutionalizing the elderly people. What forcing them to do so are the problems associated in taking care of the daily needs and adjusting with their attitudes and behaviours.

This qualitative research is focused on the family people who take care of elders at homes. The aim of the study is to understand the major problems faced by the family people in taking care of elderly people in their family. The focus of the study is to go in-depth to know the various factors which affect the smooth running of family in relation to managing olders. Therefore the objective of the study is to identify and describe the various constraints faced by family people in taking care of elderly people in their families. The study has the following implications: the research findings can be used to strength the nature and type of elderly care being provided by several functionaries; it enhances the scope for providing training and development for the care givers at home and institution; it impart the knowledge base for social work practitioner.

Introduction

> *"Men of the age object too much, consult too long, adventure too little, repent too soon and seldom drove business home to the full period, but content themselves with a mediocrity of success"*
>
> —Bacon.

The above words of Francis Bacon depict the much complaint nature of elderly persons one may find in general. These traits of elders certainly have a bearing on the care givers in their families or at institutions. Care giving arises out of the social nature of Indian family and the obligations of family members to one another. Elderly people at home contribute greatly to the family environment enriching the essence and spirit of human existence. However, they cannot contribute actively to the family in the old age and tend to think of themselves as redundant. So the need arises from the other members of the family to cater to their physical as well as emotional needs. This requires a lot of patience, immense understanding and emotional maturity at all times.

Caring for the elder is always a challenge. Sickness and ailments are something which seems to follow them and inevitably and there are crises, which may arise suddenly. The family members, in spite of regular work schedules, have to make time to take care of them and their needs. Understanding their mental makeup and learning to identify their requirements are very important aspects.

Family caregivers are responsible for the physical, emotional and often financial support of another person who is unable to care for him/herself due to illness, injury or disability. The care recipient may be a family member, life partner or friend. In the Indian family setup, the majority of family caregivers are women. The care of a family member, in the absence of a spouse, often falls on the shoulders of a daughter or daughter-in-law. Many women spend a large percentage of their adult lives caring for children and elderly family members, in addition to working outside of the home.

According to the recent statistics related to elderly people in India (Census 2001), it was observed that as many as 75% of elderly persons were living in rural areas. About 48.2% of elderly persons were women, out of whom 55% were widows. A total of 73% of elderly persons were illiterate and dependent on physical labour. One-third was reported to be living below the poverty line, i.e., 66% of older persons were in a vulnerable situation without adequate food, clothing, or shelter. About 90% of the elderly were from the unorganized sector, i.e., they have no regular source of income. India is one of the few countries in the world in which the sex ratio of the aged favours males. This could be attributed to various reasons such as under-reporting of females, especially widows and higher female mortality in different age groups.

Methodology

This exploratory study focused on the various issues faced by the caregivers in relation to managing elders. This study is qualitative research employing case study method of selected group of ten care givers by employing snowball sampling techniques. The elders taken care of by them are between 70 to 80 years. The data were collected from using close ended questions for demographic profile and interview to elicit opinions of the care givers.

Results and Discussions

The primary stressors of women who are taking care of elders are identified as: (*a*) **Monitoring** - keeping an overall vigilance over the care (*b*) **Medicating** - giving medicine at proper time (*c*) **Physical assistance -** for their personal needs and for bedding, bathing (*d*) **Feeding -** when they are hungry

The outcome of these stressors reflects in various family and personal lifestyle of the caregivers.

(*i*) ***Marital discard:*** Marital relationships suffer due to stress and lack of quality time together. The caregivers fail miserably in spending quality time with their children as well as partners. They have to sacrifice a lot of their activities for the sake of the elders and often leading to dislike for the partner and hatred for the children. In the case of daughter-in-laws taking care of the elderly parents of their partners, misunderstanding between the partners is common phenomenon.

(*ii*) ***Social isolation:*** The women who take care of elders at home fail to have regular social meetings and other outside social activities due to the engagements at home with the elders. If the caregiver is a working lady, his focus on the job itself is at stake and career development and progress become a nightmare.

(iii) ***Emotional loneliness:*** Due to loss of social contacts, many care givers are confined to their homes which in turn lead to the feeling of loneliness and the feeling of isolated from the outside world.

(iv) ***Economic strains:*** This is yet another constraint in the life of care givers who are sandwiched between their own personal, family needs and the needs of elders. The caregivers also feel that they do not do justice to their own children in satisfying their various needs and the various economic resources are directed towards the elders and their caretaking. The elders too demand various facilities for them with the claim that they earned a lot while they were active. The middle class and lower middle class people are the ones who suffer economically taking care of elders.

(v) ***Lack of appreciation:*** In majority of the cases, the increased number of complaints of the elders about the caregivers, the habitual nagging felt by the caregivers and the feeling that the care given is not appreciated by the elders lead to depression and poor motivation for the caregivers

Conclusion

The Indian elderly population is growing rapidly due to the development of science and technology especially in the healthcare system. The health care needs of the elderly have increased tremendously in the past few decades and the need for a prolonged elder care is experienced in many families. Due to the joint family system and strong cultural concept that taking care of elders is the sole responsibility of the children, many families take care of elders at home rather than entrust them to institutional care givers. This study focused on care givers at homes and identified that they have primary as well as secondary stressors in taking care of elders. Marital discord, social isolation, emotional loneliness, economic strains and lack of appreciation for the good work done are some of the major concerns of caregivers under study. When urbanization, migration to cities, disintegration of the joint family system and married couple moving out of the joint household become popular, the absence of traditional caregivers at home will create a big vacuum in the care for the elders and the elderly might become a vulnerable group, looking for care and attention in the institutionalized care-homes like the western countries.

CHAPTER

19

The Contributing Factors for Non-retirement Life Among Rural Population

A Case Study

— Ms. A. Kavitha

ABSTRACT

Retirement is the point in life where a person who laboured for few decades will stop employment completely and take rest from active work. Generally government employees retire at the age of 58 in Tamil Nadu although there are moves to raise it to 60 years. Government and other employees enjoy one or other retirement benefits in the form of pension fund, Provident Fund etc to support their retirement life. However in the rural areas it is not the case. People tend to work till they die or bedridden. Are they forced to work or work voluntarily depends upon the reasons they have for their work. However, the fact remains that they are generally abused in the families and harmed physically or emotionally whether working or non working, retired or non-retired. We rarely come across an elderly person who is not abused even verbally.

This study is aimed at identifying the contributing factors for elders at rural communities to lead a non-retirement life and the kind of abuses they face even in the situation of non-retirement life. Therefore the objectives of this study are twofold: first it explores the different contributing factors for non-retirement life among rural elders. Second, the study identifies the various abuses that take place among the elders who lead their non-retirement life.

This is a qualitative study that describes the current condition of elders in rural setting and communities. The study was conducted in the rural communities of Udumalaipettai taluk of Tirupur district, Tamil Nadu. Data will was gathered through unstructured interviews in the form of casual talks and storytelling. The specific methods of storytelling and casual talks helped the researcher to get accurate data from the rural elders who otherwise are not open to formal interviews and systematic questioning. The collected data was made into themes and categories for further discussion.

The study foresees the following benefits: it will bring to surface the various life situations of elders in rural areas. It will help sociologists, psychologists, social workers and rural development policy makers to think further on various community development programs, human and social development concerns. Finally the study will help the researcher to commit fully in to the cause of rural population as a social worker.

Introduction

Retirement is the point in life where a person who laboured for few decades stops employment completely and rest from active work or profession. Generally government employees retire at the age of 58 in Tamil Nadu although there are moves to raise it to 60 years. Employees generally enjoy one or other retirement benefits in the form of Pension Fund, Provident Fund etc to support their retirement life. However in the rural areas where people depend upon their own farming and other small businesses tend to work till they die or bedridden. Although apparently one may presume that the elderly people are abused physically or psychologically, their words and cries are not taken to the stage. Particularly the problems and sufferings of elders surviving in rural areas are not generally noticeable or not seriously taken for consideration. Therefore, this study on the non-retirement life among rural population brings the heart saying of rural elders to the limelight.

This study focuses on two major aspects of elderly people in the rural areas, mainly: what are the different contributing factors for non-retirement life among rural elders; second, the study identifies the various abuses that take place among the elders who lead their non-retirement life. This study is an indicator of exhibiting sufferings and psychological feelings of rural elderly people, mainly farmers. Are they forced to work or work voluntarily depends upon the reasons they have their work. However, the fact remains that they are generally abused in families and harmed physically or emotionally whether working or non working, retired or non-retired.

This is a qualitative study that describes the current condition of elders in rural setting and communities. The study was conducted in the rural communities of Ravanapuram village, Udumalpet taluk of Tirupur district, Tamil Nadu. Data were collected from 24 elderly people and random sampling method was used to collect data. Out of 24 samples, 6 were couples, 6 widows and 6 widowers. They were in the age bracket of 61 to 70 years. They belong to middle class and Konguvellar community. Data were gathered through unstructured interviews in the form of casual talks and storytelling. The specific method of storytelling and casual talks helped the researcher to get the accurate data from the rural elders who otherwise are not open or shy to formal interviews and systematic questioning. The collected data were made into themes and categories for future discussion as per the qualitative research norms.

The researcher collected data from June 2 to June 29, 2010. The researcher met the farmers by visiting them in their working places and asked about their health conditions and started talking about their work and other conditions of life. After having 15-20 minutes of casual discussion, the researcher asked about the reason for their non-retirement life bit by bit. From this kind of informal conversation and storytelling methods the data was collected by the researcher.

The data from storytelling and informal conversations provided sufficient material for analyzing data qualitatively. A theoretical editing analysis protocol was used to develop conceptual themes from the data (Strauss & Corbin, 1990). It was done in the following way: first, the researcher identified meaningful segments into patterns. In the second step, triangulation was done by investigator independently to categorize he data into provisional themes and categories. In the third stage, the themes and categories were re-examined by the researcher and conceptual themes categories were formed.

Results and Discussion

The study results identify that it is not a single factor that contributes to the non-retirement life among elder population in the study area rather it is multifaceted. The following are the identified factors that contribute to the non-retirement life among rural population.

Lack of Financial support: Finance is the most essential thing in all of our life. Human gets money as a reward for their service. Generally when people retire from jobs they depend upon others for their financial support whether depend on their children or either on Institutions they worked or sometimes on savings. In the rural setting and among farmers, it is not the case. Working as farmers they have no retirement scheme or pension money to support their future. They also have very poor saving system. So they remain as non-retired workers. Apart from their basic needs, they look for financial assistance for the following:

(*a*) *To meet their family obligations:* As the elderly person to the family they have certain obligations such as giving money to their daughter, grand children during important functional/festival occasions.

(*b*) *Repay their debts:* Most of the people have no support from their children to take up the burden of repaying their parent's or family debts. In such case the elders has to continue their responsibility in repaying their borrowings.

(*c*) *For medical expenses:* As the elderly people have no savings, they need medical assistance that is common in the old age. As they are often not taken care of by their own children, they depend upon themselves.

Terror of Abuse: Elders get abuse when they are unable to support their family. With fear on abuse the rural farmers continuing to work for survival.

Abandoned Responsibilities: Rural-Urban migration plays an important factor for non-retire life among rural population. Because of migration the children abandon their parents and do not take care of their parents. Hence rural elders were in the situation to carry out their children and relatives responsibilities.

Dignity and Independent: Every man feels that they have dignity and independent until they under working and earning. Rural elders have the motto of leading life with dignity and being independent and so they have no interest in getting their retire life.

Self-fulfilment: Most of the people work in the farms starts their work from later childhood. So it is hard for them to take rest without working in the land. Working in the farmland has become part of their personality and life-style. This study observes that rural elders continuing their non-retirement life especially for this self-fulfilment also. Thereby they were avoiding the boredom of being lazy or lonely.

Avoid Inadequate/Incapability: The feeling of worthlessness starts at the time of depending on others in satisfying their needs. Hence to avoid the feeling of inadequate tendency and incapability hey ready to carry on their work. The above stated factors are the main contributors for the non-retirement life of rural population. These factors were the commonly observed reasons that generally happening in every rural population.

The following are the general abuses identified among non-retired elders:

Physical abuses: Depriving the older person from having food with the aim of punishing them and expose them to harsh weather are the major physical abuses. Beating (with stick, rope), kicking, slapping are other forms of physical abuses.

Financial/Material abuses: Taking over of assets and property and the use of funds belonging to the elderly under false pretence, forging of any kind of document to dupe the older person are commonly seen financial abuses. Demanding from the elders to get expensive and inappropriate gift items are another form of abuse prevalent in the rural area.

Psychological/Emotional abuses: Terrorizing or menacing the older person by way of not allowing them to take care of their grand children and ignoring them in family/social functions. These kinds of psychological abuse lead them to depression, hopelessness, helplessness, and thoughts of suicide.

Prevention/Intervention Strategies

The level of awareness on the plight of the elderly is low. It should be deliberate and concerted effort through education of younger generation as well as educating the people to have enough savings for their old age. This will in turn change the attitudes of individuals and the society to the special needs and challenges of the elderly. Since many of the abuses and ill-treatments are happening inside the family it gets unreported. It is therefore the need of the time to direct the attention of the society and social work agencies to the phenomenon of elder abuse. Create and sustain program that will assist the abused, and abuser in prevention and intervention strategies that will benefit all in the society. In short, educating the younger generation to respect the human rights of elders and preparing the adults for retirement life are the major prevention strategies one can think of in helping the elders in the rural areas.

Conclusion

The result of the study is the photograph of rural elders life especially those who leading non-retire life. The study has identified various issues and concerns of elders in rural areas. The different kinds of abuses and the situation that lead to the life of elders in the rural communities will help sociologists, psychologists, social workers and rural development policy makers to think further on various community development programs, human and social development concerns. Finally it is foreseen that the study will help the researcher to commit fully in to the cause of rural population as a social worker.

REFERENCES

Allen, P. B., W. E. Field, and M. J. Frick. (1995). Assessment of Work-Related Injury Risk for Farmers and Ranchers with Physical Disabilities. *Journal of Agricultural Safety and Health* 1 (2): 71-81.

Bhattacharya, Dhires.1989. *A Concise History of Indian Economy*, New Delhi: Prentice-Hall.

Coward, Raymond T. and Gary R. Lee (eds.) (1985). *The Elderly in Rural Society*. New York: Springer Publishing Co.

Kaur, Raminderjeet. (2008). "Assessment of genetic damage in the workers occupationally exposed to various pesticides in selected districts of Punjab", unpublished PhD thesis, Department of Human Biology, Punjabi University, Patiala.

Irudaya Rajan S (2003.). Demography of ageing. In: Dey AB, editor. *Ageing in India, Situational analysis and planning for the future*. New Delhi: Rakmo Press.

Kartikeyan S, Pedhambkar BS, Jape MR (1999). Social security the Global Scenario. *Indian Journal of Occupational Health*; 42:91.8.

Khandelwal SK, (2003). Mental health of older people. In: Dey AB, editor. *Ageing in India. Situational analysis and planning for the future*. New Delhi: Rakmo Press

Kulshreshtha, S. (2009). *Social Security for Elderly in India* , merinews.com

Meeta and Rajivlochan (2006). *Farmers suicide: facts and possible policy interventions*, Yashada, Pune, pp. 11-13.

Morbidity, Health Care and Condition of the Aged. *National Sample Survey 60th Round* (January to June 2004). Government of India, March 2006. p. 54.65.

Purty AJ, Bazroy J, Kar M, Vasudevan K, Veliath A, Panda P. (2006). Morbidity Pattern among the elderly population in the rural area of Tamil Nadu, *Indian. Journal of Medical Science* 36:45.50.

Rao Venkoba A (1984). Health care of rural aged. New Delhi: Indian Council of Medical Research.

Reddy PH (1996). The health of the aged in India. *Health Transit Rev*;6:233.44.

Vijaya Kumar S. Edit. (1995). *Challenges before the elderly: An Indian scenario*. New Delhi: M.D. Publications

PART III

Old People's Perspective of Managing the Old Age

— Dr. Mini. T. C.

ABSTRACT

It is a known fact that the population ageing is a universal event, omnipresent, touching everybody at one stage of life. Ageing is a continuing reality that cannot be retrieved or taken back - we will not return to the young age once biological growth takes place. The pace and process of change differs greatly from country to country and culture to culture. Therefore a culture-specific study of ageing and its personal and social implications have profound impact in understanding, adjusting and living the unavoidable fact of human aging.

Elderly people are expected to be among the most prominent global demographic trends of the 21st century. This is a direct consequence of the ongoing global fertility transition (decline) and of mortality decline at older ages due to major technological developments in the field of genetic engineering, understanding the causes and cure of sickness. These lead to many socio-economic and health consequences, including the increase in the old-age dependency ratio (UN, 2002).

It is obvious that managing old age is a complex issue in many respects. Like other traditional societies, the State of Kerala has cultural values and traditional practices which emphasize that the elderly members of the family are to be treated with honour and respect. The families of the elderly people are expected to ensure the needed care and support for the aged. However, the recent changes in the size and structure of families have caused role changes and functional alterations in the families leading to a threat to the traditional concept of respect and acceptance of elders at families.

This research is aimed at knowing the perspectives of elderly people - how they manage the old age and how they view the younger generation should prepare themselves to face old age in the future. The data is gathered by means of informal interviews in the way of casual conversations, story-telling methods from Pambadumpara rural panchayath situated in Idukki district of Kerala State. The subjects consist of 58 elderly people, age ranging from 65 to 78 years. Field notes gathered are written down and a content analysis is done as per the permitted norms of qualitative analysis.

Results of the study imply that the elderly people in Kerala face three major kinds of adjustment problems. They are i) pitiable economic adjustment leading to complete dependence on their sons and daughter-in laws; ii) poor vocational adjustment leading to lack of pass time activities; and iii) pathetic family and social adjustment having regular mutual quarrels and clashes on values together with lack of respect and acceptance.

The study findings also reveal that the attitude of younger generation towards the elders call for a total change of mindset and preparedness from the part of the elders in order to feel at ease at old age. Economical security, preparedness for old age in the form of old age activities and, to a greater extent open mindset to accept the changing value system of youngsters, can safeguard a person when they reach old age.

Introduction

Ageing is an inevitable process which every human being has to go through. Population aging has many important socio-economic and health consequences, including the increase in the old-age dependency ratio. Ageing of population presents challenges for public health (concerns over possible bankruptcy of Medicare and related programs) as well as for economic development (shrinking and aging of labour force, possible bankruptcy of social security systems) (Gavrilov & Heuveline, 2003). Geriatrics has not yet been developed as a branch of Medicare in many parts of the country.

Elder abuse and neglect is a day-to-day phenomenon all over the world and India is not an exception. The organisations like WHO, UNFPA and WHO_CIG have done a lot of research projects in the area of elderly abuse and came with the slogan in 1991 " To add life to the years that have been added to life". This slogan highlights the neglected case of elders in our country. The Madrid International Plan of Action on Ageing (MIPAA, UN, 2002) has several implications to address the issue of elder abuse. It calls for changes in attitudes, policies and practices at all levels and in all sectors in order to ensure that people everywhere are able to age with security and dignity, as citizens with full rights. Also, it suggests that there is an urgent need to expand educational opportunities in the fields of geriatrics and gerontology.

Table 20.1 : Socio-demographic indicators in Kerala and India

Socio-demographic indicators	Kerala	India
Infant Mortality Rate (IMR)	14	58
Total Fertility Rate (TFR)	1.9	2.7
Under-5 Child Mortality	3.0	17.3
Life expectancy at birth (e^0_0)	74.0	63.5
Aging Index	40.2	21.1
Per cent older adults (age 60+)	10.5	7.4

So, the socio-economic and emotional aspects of the aged population are also worthwhile concern. The changing age structure due to momentum will favour a higher old age dependency ratio. In this aspect also the state intervention will become absolutely necessary and unavoidable in the case of Kerala (Sadasivan Nair, 2010). Table 20.1 above provides a highlight of the statistical data on socio-demographic variables in Kerala and India.

We can observe from the above data that the life expectancy of people in Kerala is very high, just like the situation in Western countries. The living arrangements have its own significance on health and well-being of older populations, particularly in traditional societies such as Kerala. Traditionally, younger generations are supposed to take responsibility of their older counterparts in the house. In addition to fulfilling basic daily requirements, younger generations were used to provide emotional, social and mental support to their previous generations. Rapid urbanization and movement of younger generations from their home in the

Table 20.2 : Census of India, Reports; and Population Projections for Kerala

Year	Population aged 60 +(in millions)		
	Total	Male	Female
1961	0.9	.4	.5
1971	1.3	.6	.7
1981	1.9	.9	1.0
1986	2.2	1.0	1.2
1991	2.6	1.1	1.5
1996	3.1	1.3	1.7
2001	3.5	1.5	2.0
2006	4.0	1.7	2.2
2011	4.6	2.0	2.6
2016	5.7	2.6	3.1
2021	6.9	3.2	3.7
2026	8.3	3.9	4.4

search of career advancement have tended to weaken traditional systems and ancestral values in Indian societies (Bhat *et al.*, 2001; Chanana & Talwar, 1987; Pal, 2004; Prakash, 2007; Shah, 1999). Consequently, disabilities were reported to be more pronounced among older adults living without their spouses. At the same time, level of health care utilization was lower among them compared with those living with spouses (Gopal Agrawal, Kunal Keshri & Kirti Gaur, 2009).

Table 20.2 gives the population of 60+ people in the state of Kerala during 1961-2026 actual figures. The 60+ population has increased more than 3 times of that of 1961 figures by 1996 and we can see further increment in this sect of population for 2026.

In the light of these statistical facts we can understand that a study of old people in Kerala is very much essential and worth doing. Accordingly we have taken up this study on the perspectives of managing of old age from the view point of elders.

Objectives of the Study

The main objectives of the study are: To know the perspectives of elderly people on how they manage old age; to know of their view point on how they want the younger generation to prepare themselves to face the old age in future

Methodology

This is a qualitative ethnographic research in which the author informally talked with the participants with some guide questions and collected data on the perspectives of elders. The data was collected from 58 elderly people in the age group of 65-78 years from Pambadumpara panchayath situated in Idukki district of Kerala State. Field notes are prepared and content analysis is done as per the norms of qualitative Dresearch.

Table 20.3: The Demography of the Study Area

	No. of households	Total population	Males	Females
Pampadumpara Panchayath	5,247	22,548	11,178	11,370

Table 20.4: The Literacy of Subjects in Percentage

	Male	Female
Literates	20	23
Illiterates	7	8

Table 20.5: The Marital Status of Subjects

Marital status	No. of respondents
Single	3
Married	38
widowed	12
Divorced/Separated	5

Results and Discussion

The responses were collected in the form of narrations and stories regarding the problems faced by elders in the society and how they perceive that can be avoided. We also tried to find out whether they were able to manage old age on their own. Also their suggestion as the message to younger generation on how they can prepare to age in future in a graceful manner is taken down. Themes evolved from the findings reveal the major problems of elderly people.

Major problems of elders as they see it:

i. Feel economically deprived

ii. Feel that youngsters consider them as a burden

iii. They are not fed on time

iv. Not treated with respect

v. Old vessels are used to give them food
vi. Lack of good clothing
vii. No gold ornaments are given
viii. Often physically and verbally abused for requesting minimal comforts
ix. Abused for talking to guests
x. Verbally and physically abused for asking for food in time
xi. Feeling of loneliness and separation (as if living in a jail)
xii. No respect grand children
xiii. Separate table/place is allotted for eating food and no place with family members
xiv. No timely medical help and has to suffer in silence
xv. Not permitted to talk to anyone
xvi. Not allowed to go out of the house

These evolved themes give us a picture of the elderly people inside their own families and the evidences reveal that elders are continually being abused by their family members/ caretakers at homes.

Perception of Old Age and the Current Reality: The subjects of the study feel that old age is a period of rest and relaxation. However, in reality it is not so. Sometimes they are burdened by the family members and many a times they are not able to relax as they desire. They also expect that old age is the time to get respect from younger generation, but in fact they are insulted. Elderly people expect the family to consult and get their opinion in each and every matters regarding major decision making in the house, but they are completely ignored.

Managing Old Age: The elderly people cope up with their current problems and challenges in an unhealthy way. Mainly they cope with the situation by way of complaining, murmuring, crying, praying and suffering in silence. They would be happy to look for some forum to report or inform their abuses but they are not able due to the rural setup. In short, they are not able to manage their old age in a healthy manner. However, they suggest that having some economic security, some good friends near their homes to ventilate the pain and some leisure time activities to get minimal income as well as to kill the time usefully is the ideal coping for old age which they are deprived off due to lack of preparation.

Lack of Preparation for Old Age: One of the major issues identified in this study was that the elders are not prepared to this kind of life-style at old age and they never expected that they will be in this miserable situation. So lack of real preparedness to old age cause them enormous amount of pain and agony. Many of them expressed that only proper preparation to face old age in various forms can help elderly people to manage this life situation. Thus the study results lead us to the inevitable fact that elders in the society do not manage their old age well.

Major Adjustment Needed: The study also classifies the adjustment problems faced by the elderly people of the study area into three categories: they are i) economic adjustments ii) space adjustment at home and other family adjustments and iii) social adjustments.

All the three identified adjustment areas, one or another, closely related to their lack of preparedness for old age. In the Indian scenario, people save money for their children and invest it for the welfare of their children and fail to look at their own retirement plans. Although this situation is changing in the urban areas, the study results in the rural area give a picture of economically helpless elders. The space and related issues at homes reveal that fact that the elders would like to interfere in each and every issue and problems in the house whereas the younger generation does not like it. Also ill-treatment from the part of in-laws and grandchildren are serious concerns damaging the value system in our society. The lack of social adjustment in the old age too reveals the fact that the elders are not fully prepared for their old age by having some sort of friend circles and other hobby networks.

Conclusion

The study concludes that the elders currently in the rural Kerala do not manage their old age properly. The elders have their own perception of old which they fail to achieve due to various reasons. One major reason would be lack of preparation from the part of the elders themselves. The study also suggests a total mindset change for both the elders as well as youngsters for facing the phenomena of old age. Preparedness for old age in the form of economical security, old age activities, and open mindset to accept the changing value system of youngsters may safeguard a person when they reach old age.

REFERENCES

Agrawal, G., and Arokiasamy, P. (2009). Morbidity Prevalence and Health Care Utilization among Older Adults in India. *Journal of Applied Gerontology*. First published online on July 22, 2009.

Bhat, A.K., and Dhruvarajan, R. (2001). Ageing in India: Drifting Intergenerational Relations, Challenges and Options. *Ageing & Society*, 21: 621-640.

Bose, A., and M. K. Shankardass. (2004). *Growing Old in India: Voices Reveal, Statistics Speak*. Delhi: B. R. Publication Corporation.

Chanana, H.B., and Talwar, P.P. (1987). Aging in India: Its Socio-economic and Health Implications. *Asia-Pacific Population Journal*, 2 (3): 23-38.

Dadkhah, A. (2009). Service Framework for Older People in Japan: A Guideline for Asian Countries. *Middle East Journal of Age and Ageing*. 6 (3): 18-22.

Harper, S. (2006). *Ageing Societies: Myths, Challenges and Opportunities*. New York: Oxford University Press.

Heikkinen, E., (2003). *What are the Main Risk Factors for Disability in Old Age and How can Disability be Prevented*? Copenhagen, WHO Regional Office for Europe (Health Evidence Network report).

Khaw, K.T. (1997). Epidemiological Aspects of Ageing. Philosophical Transactions: *Biological Sciences*. 352 (1363): 1829-1835.

Khetarpal, K., Soneja, S., and Kumar, V. (1996). Physical and Neuropsychiatric Impairment Amongst the Aged and Their Relationship to Socio-economic Status. In V. Kumar (Ed.), *Aging-Indian Perspective and Global Scenario*. (134-136). New Delhi: AIIMS.

Konjengbam, S., N. Bimol, J. Singh, E. V. Devi, & M. Singh. (2007). Disabilities in ADL Among the Ederly in an Urban Area of Manipur. *IJPMR* 18 (2): 41-43.

Kumar, V. (2003). Health Status and Health Care Services among Older Persons in India. *Journal of Aging & Social Policy*, 15(2/3): 67-83.

Medhi, G. K., and J. Mahanta. (2007). Population Ageing in India: Health Promotion through Life Course Approach. *Current Science*. 93 (8): 1046.

Murabito, J. M., M. J. Pencina, L. Zhu, M. K. Hayes, and P. Shrader. (2008). Temporal Trends in Self-Reported Functional Limitations and Physical Disabilities among the Community-Dwelling Elderly Population: The Framingham Heart Study. *American Journal of Public Health. 98 (7): 1256-1262.*

Pandey, M. K. (2009). *Poverty and Disability among Elderly in India: Evidences from Household Survey.* Delhi: Institute of Economic Growth.

Prevalence among the Highest Income Groups of Older Brazilians. *American Journal of Public Health*. 99 (1): 81-92.

Prakash, I. J., (2003). Ageing, Disability and Disabled Older People in India. In *An ageing India: Perspecitve, Prospects and Policies*, I. P. S. Liebig and S. I. Rajan (eds.). New Delhi: Rawat Publications.

Prakash, S. (2007). Policies and Programmes on Population Ageing: Indian Perspective. Presented in Seminar on the *Social, Health and Economic Consequences of Population Ageing in the Context of Changing Families*, Bangkok.

Sengupta, M., and Agree, E.M. (2003). Gender, Health, Marriage and Mobility Difficulty among Older Adults in India. *Asia Pacific Population Journal*. 18 (4): 53-65.

Shah, A.M. (1999). Changes in the Family and the Elderly. *Economic and Political Weekly*, 34(20): 1179-82.

Shah, B., and A. K. Prabhakar. (1997). Chronic Morbidity Profile among Elderly. *Indian Journal of Medical Research*. 106: 265-272.

Smith, J.P. (2007). The Impact of Social Economic Status on Health over the Life-Course. *Journal of Human Resources*. 42: 739-764.

Sobba, I., and M. S. N. Reddy. (2006). *Health Ageing: Concept, Problems and Prospects. In Older Persons in India*, ed. A. K. Joshi. New Delhi: Serials Publications.

United Nations. (2002). World Population Ageing: 1950-2050. In Department of Economic and Social Affairs. New York: Population Division.

CHAPTER 21

Stress Management of the Elderly

— Meena
— Dr. V. Darling Selvi

ABSTRACT

Elderly population is subjected to stress through various forms of abuses. The abuses may be in the form of Physical, Financial, Neglect, Poor Health and the like. An abuser can be a spouse, partner, relative, a friend or neighbour, a volunteer worker, a paid worker, practitioner, solicitor or any other individual with the intent to deprive a vulnerable person of their resources. Relatives include adult children and their spouses or partners, their offspring and other extended family members. Stress can be a cause for both mental and physical agony. This paper attempts to analyze the stressors causing stress among the elderly. For the purpose of the study, an interview questionnaire has been administered among fifty elders who lead a stressful life. Hypotheses have been framed and tested in this connection through Chi Square test. The researchers concluded that a loving care, proper health management, balanced diet and the like will help the elders to get rid of their stress and paves way to their successful and peaceful living in their old age.

Introduction

Population aging is a worldwide phenomenon. Census reports indicate that the Indian population has approximately tripled during the last 50 years, but the number of elderly Indians has increased more than fourfold. When considering the continuation of the trend, the United Nations predicts that the Indian population will again grow by 50 per cent in the next 50 years, whereas the elderly population is expected to grow another fourfold. The Indian population has increased from 361 million in 1951 to 1.027 billion in 2001. Simultaneously, the number of older people has increased from 19 million (4 per cent of total population) to 77 million (7.5 per cent of the total) during the same time span (Registrar General of India). In order to study the implications of an aging population in India, the changing Indian demographic configuration needs to be highlighted first. That will help us assess the challenges to be met in the future.

Stress can be defined as a state of physical and mental tension caused by certain external or internal factors in a person's life. The art of stress management is to keep one at a level of stimulation that is healthy and enjoyable. Life without stimulus would be incredibly dull and boring. Life with too much stimulus becomes unpleasant and tiring, and may ultimately damage your health or well-being. Too much stress can seriously interfere with your ability to perform effectively. By analyzing the likely causes of stress, you will be able to plan your responses to likely forms of stress. The mind's reaction to stress is harder to predict. These mental reactions vary according to the situation and the person. They may include feelings of anger, fear, anxiety, annoyance or frustration. Prolonged stress is a serious condition can lead to life threatening illnesses particularly high blood pressure, stroke and heart attacks. Managing stress is all about taking charge: taking charge of your thoughts, your emotions, your schedule, your environment, and the way you deal with problems. The ultimate goal is a balanced life, with time for work, relationships, relaxation, and fun – plus the resilience to hold up under pressure and meet challenges head on. A survey which has been conducted among 25 elder people in Kanyakumari District of Tamil Nadu during the month of June 2010 has revealed from Table 21.1.

Table 21.1 : Personal Profile of the Sample Respondents

Variables	Frequency	Per cent	Cumulative Per cent
1	2	3	4
Age			
60-65	4	16	16
66-70	8	32	48
71-75	5	20	68
76-80	6	24	92
81-85	2	8	100
Total	25	100	
Sex			
Male	15	60	60
Female	10	40	100
Total	25	100	
Marital Status			
Married	12	48	48
Unmarried	0	0	48
Deserted	0	0	48
Widow	8	32	80
Widower	5	20	100
Total	25	100	
Qualification			
School	3	12	12
Degree	15	60	72
PG	3	12	84

1	2	3	4
Professional	4	16	100
Total	25	100	
Employment Status			
Working	5	20	20
Retired	12	48	68
Housewives	8	32	100
Total	25	100	
Employed after Retirement			
Yes	5	20	20
No	20	80	100
Total	25	100	
Nature of Employment			
Government	18	72	72
Private	7	28	100
Total	25	100	
Mode of living			
Single	3	12	12
Family	20	80	92
Old age homes	2	8	100
Total	25	100	
No. of dependents			
Nil	20	80	80
1-3	5	20	100
Total	25	100	
Nature of residence			
Own	23	92	92
Leased	0	0	92
Rented	2	8	100
Total	25	100	

Source: Primary Survey

Out of the sample respondents, 48 per cent belong to the age group of 60 to 70, 44 per cent between 71 and 80, and 8 percent above 85 years, consist of 60 per cent male and 40 percent female, 48 per cent are Married, 32 per cent are widows and 20 per cent are widowers. The sample group consist of well qualified persons with 60 per cent degree holders, 12 per cent have completed their school studies and post graduation, 48 per cent have retired from services, 20 percent are still working and 32 per cent are housewives, 20 percent hold the job even after retirement, 72 per cent have the experience of working in government services, and 28 percent in private concerns, 80 per cent had the privilege of living with the family, 12 per cent lead their life alone while 8 percent lead their life in the old age homes. Among them, 80 percent have no dependents to support while 20 per cent have to support of one to three, 92 per cent had own houses while 8 percent live in rented houses.

Table 21.2 : Social Status of the Elderly

Variables	Yes	No	%
1	2	3	4
Privileges			
Traveling concessions in Roadways	-	25	0
Traveling concessions in Airways	10	15	40
Traveling concessions in Train	25	-	100
Higher, interest rates in banks, post offices	25	-	100
Tax benefits	20	5	80
Priority in hospitals	1	24	4
Priority in getting telephone connection	1	24	4
Food & Public Distribution	-	25	0

1	2	3	4
Old age Pension Scheme	25	-	100
Maintenance from Children	2	23	8
Total	109	141	77
Social Status			
Membership in Self Help Group	3	22	12
Senior Citizens Association	-	25	0
Membership in Temple/ Church committees	5	20	20
Membership in Cultural Associations	-	25	0
Membership in Political Parties	-	25	0
Membership in Literary Associations	1	24	4
Membership in Consumer Associations	1	24	4
Membership in Service organizations	3	22	12
Member in any other social Organizations	4	21	16
Total	17	208	8

Source: Primary Survey

Majority of the sample respondents have the privilege of enjoying travelling through train, getting more interest on their savings, food and public distribution, pension schemes and tax benefits. A few have travelled through airways. Out of the sample respondents, 77 percent have got the benefit of utilizing the various privileges available to them. The social involvement of the elderly is very low with just 8 percent participation in various social activities and at the same time the social support for them is good (Table 21.2).

Table 21.3 : Old Age Problems of Elderly

Variables	Yes	No	%
Problems			
Health	25	-	100
Loneliness	20	5	80
Financial	3	22	12
Dependents	2	23	8
Family problems	20	5	80
Insecurity	3	22	12
Abuses			
Physical	10	15	40
Mental	25	-	100
Sexual	-	25	0
Financial	5	25	20
Attitude towards old age			
Old age has affected day-to-day life	8	17	32
Feel neglected by family members	12	13	48
Feel a burden to family	10	15	40
Not happy in life	5	20	20
Feel they are not loved by family members	6	19	24
Diseases			
Hypertension	21	4	84
Diabetics	15	15	60
Osteoarthritis	12	13	48
Bronchial asthma	5	20	20
Disability	7	18	28
Status of mobility			
Confined to the bed	3	22	12
Confined to the house	9	16	36
Completely mobile	15	15	60
Partially mobile	5	2	20

Source: Primary Survey

Almost all the elderly persons were affected by the health problems, 80 per cent with loneliness and Family problems, 12 per cent each with Financial and Insecurity and a few because of dependents. With regards to the abuses, mental agony is the most prevalent which is followed by Physical, and Financial, and none is affected by the Sexual harassment. The attitude towards old age differs from person to person. As much as 48 percent Feel neglected by family members, 40 per cent feel burden to family, 32 of the old aged were percent Old age has affected day-to-day life, 24 per cent feel they are not loved by family members, 20 per cent feel that they are not happy in life. Diseases are the most acute problem which affects the elderly people very often. Among the common diseases, 84 percent are affected by Hypertension, 60 per cent by Diabetes, 48 per cent by Osteoarthritis, and 20 percent by Bronchial asthma (Table 21.3).

Table 21.4 : Behavioural Changes

Particulars	Yes	No	%
1	2	3	4
Expresses anger, frustration, or exhaustion	20	5	80
Isolates the elder from the outside world, friends, or relatives	21	4	84
Obviously lacks care giving skills	20	5	80
Is unreasonably critical and / or dissatisfied with social and health care providers and changes providers frequently	16	9	64
Refuses to apply for economic aid or services for the elder and resists outside help	17	8	68
Exhibits emotional distress such as crying, depression, or despair	19	6	76

1	2	3	4
Has nightmares or difficulty sleeping	21	4	44
Sudden loss of appetite that is unrelated to a medical condition	-	25	0
Is confused and disoriented	20	5	80
Is emotionally numb, withdrawn, or detached	21	4	84
Exhibits regressive behaviour	22	3	88
Malnutrition	-	25	0
Exhibits regressive behaviour	-	25	0
Exhibits fear toward the caregiver	7	18	28
Expresses unrealistic expectations about their care	6	19	24
Trembling, clinging, cowering, lack of eye contact	7	18	28
Agitation	3	22	12
Hyper vigilance	-	25	0
Evasiveness	4	21	16
Ambivalence, deference, passivity, shame	22	3	88
Anxiety (mild to severe)	24	1	96
Depression, hopelessness, helplessness, thoughts of suicide	25	-	100
Confusion, disorientation	25	-	100
Traumatic or post traumatic stress	-	25	0
Family counselling to resolve or mediate conflicts and address tensions or stresses that give rise to abuse or neglect	-	25	0

Source: Primary Survey

Depression, hopelessness, helplessness, thoughts of suicide, Confusion, disorientation (100%), Anxiety (96%), Exhibits regressive behaviour (88%), Isolation from the outside world, friends, or relatives (84%), emotionally numb, withdrawn, or detached (84%), Expresses anger, frustration, or exhaustion (80%), Obviously lacks care giving skills (80%), confused and disoriented (80%), Exhibits emotional distress such as crying, depression, or despair (76%), Refuses to apply for economic aid or services for the elder and resists outside help (68%), and dissatisfied with social and health care providers and changes providers frequently (64%) are the behavioural changes which occurs during the old age (Table 21.3).

Table 21.5 : Consequences of stress

Particulars	Yes	No	%
1	2	3	4
Irritation	21	4	84
Boredom	18	7	72
Depression	20	5	80
Reduced Job satisfaction	2	23	8
Lack of Memory	21	4	84
Poor Judgment	17	8	68
Lower self esteem	20	5	80
Negative attitude	24	1	96
Lack of self confidence	23	2	92
Anxiety	4	21	16
Fatigue	18	7	72
Voluntary retirement	20	5	80
Absence	20	5	80
Accident Prone	16	9	64
Drug addiction	11	14	44
Consequences of stress on work			
Loss of originality	20	5	80

1	2	3	4
Reduced efficiency	21	4	84
Reduced capacity	22	3	88
Reduced interest in work	20	5	80
Increased rigidity	20	5	80
Dampened initiative	20	5	80
Pending work accumulation	19	6	76
Unusual delay	21	4	84

Source: Primary Survey

Stress is the common phenomenon to the people of all age group especially to old age people. Their consequences are many which reflects in various ways. Due to stress, the elder people develop Negative attitude (96%), Lack self confidence (92%), develop Irritation (84%), Lack Memory (84%), Depression (80%), They also face problems like Lower self esteem (80%), Voluntary retirement (80%), getting Absence from the work (80%), feel Boredom (72%), and Fatigue (72%), Poor Judgment (68%), Accident proneness (64%), Drug addiction (44%), Anxiety (16%), and Reduced Job satisfaction (8%). Due to stress, the elderly has reduced physical and mental capacity (88%), reduced efficiency (84%), unusual delay (84%), Loss of originality (80%), reduced interest in work (80%), increased rigidity (80%), Dampened initiative (80%), and More work pending work accumulation (76%) (Table 21.5).

Table 21.6 : Management of Stress

Particulars	Yes	No	%
1	2	3	4
Develop a positive attitude	18	7	72
Accept life as it is	19	6	76
Set reasonable goals in life	20	5	80
Maintain a healthy diet	17	8	68
Consult with others	20	5	80

1	2	3	4
Forgetting the cause	21	4	84
Develop some hobbies	20	5	80
Develop methods to organize and to adhere	0	25	0
Avoiding people who cause stress	20	5	80
Practicing regular exercise	0	25	0
Prefer alternative work schedule	0	25	0
Resistance	21	4	84
Television	23	2	92
Computer	0	25	0
Games	2	23	8
Visiting places	1	24	4
Reading	18	7	72
Prayer	20	5	80
Meditation	19	6	76
Seeking comfort	20	5	80
Development of pleasant mental image	17	8	68
Soothing with music	20	5	80

Source: Primary Survey

The major stress relievers for the elderly is watching television (92%), forgetting the cause (84%), Resistance (84%), Set reasonable goals in life (80%), Consult with others (80%), Develop some hobbies (80%), Avoiding people who cause stress (80%), Prayer (80%), Soothing with music (80%), Accepting life as it is (76%), Meditation (76%), develop the habit of Reading (72%), Develop a positive attitude (72%), Development of pleasant mental image (68%). Games and visiting places are not much practiced by the elderly people. Further, Developing methods to organize and to adhere,

Practicing regular exercise, Preferring alternative work schedule, and the usage of Computers are completely absent among the elderly people (Table 21.6).

H_0: There is no significant difference between the consequences of stress and the management of stress

Table 21.7: Testing Hypothesis through Man – Whitney Test

Consequences of stress	Scores	R_1	Management of stress	Scores	R_2
1	2	3	4	5	6
Irritation	21	34.5	Develop a positive attitude	18	11.5
Boredom	18	11.5	Accept life as it is	19	15
Depression	20	24	Set reasonable goals in life	20	24
Reduced Job satisfaction	2	2.5	Maintain a healthy diet	17	8
Lack of Memory	21	34.5	Consult with others	20	24
Poor Judgement	17	8	Forgetting the cause	21	34.5
Lower self-esteem	20	24	Develop some hobbies	20	24
Negative attitude	24	41	Avoiding people who cause stress	20	24
Lack of self-confidence	23	39.5	Resistance	21	34.5
Anxiety	4	4	Television	23	39.5
Fatigue	18	11.5	Games	2	2.5
Voluntary retirement	20	24	Visiting places	1	1
Absence	20	24	Reading	18	11.5
Accident Prone	16	6	Prayer	20	24
Drug addiction	11	5	Meditation	19	15

1	2	3	4	5	6
Loss of originality	20	24	Seeking comfort	20	24
Reduced efficiency	21	34.5	Development of pleasant mental image	17	8
Reduced capacity	22	38	Soothing with music	20	24
Reduced interest in work	20	24			
Increased rigidity	20	24			
Dampened initiative	20	24			
More work pending	19	15			
Unusual delay	21	34.5			
Total		512			349

Source: Primary Survey

$$|Z| = \frac{U - \frac{n_1 n_2}{2}}{\sqrt{\frac{n_1 n_2 (n_1 + n_2)}{12}}} = 6\,27, U = n_1 n_2 + \frac{n_1 (n_1 + 1)}{2} - R_1 = 236$$

As the table value of Z at 5% is 1.96 which is lesser than the calculated value of Z, the stated hypothesis has been rejected and so it can be concluded that there is significant difference between the consequences of stress and the management of stress. The elderly people have different perceptions on stress and its management.

Conclusion

There are several ways of coping with stress. Some techniques of time management may help a person to control stress. In the face of high demands, effective stress management involves learning to set limits and to say "No" to some demands that others make. Managing stress is all about taking charge: taking charge of the thoughts, emotions, schedule, environment, and the way to deal with problems. The ultimate goal is a balanced life, with time for work, relationships, relaxation, and fun – plus the resilience to hold up under pressure and meet challenges head on. Stress can manifest itself in both a positive when the situation offers and opportunity for one to gain something. Stress is said to be negative when it is associated with constraints and demand. Stress is high when there is uncertainty of outcome and outcome is significant. The survey reveals the fact that the sample elder people are prove to different stressors and follow various strategies to overcome the stress. Proper planning and execution of activities will hold them up in their life and help them to lead a peaceful and successful life.

Suggestions

- **Exercise Regularly.** Physical activity plays a key role in reducing and preventing the effects of stress. Make time for at least 30 minutes of exercise, three times per week. Nothing beats aerobic exercise for releasing pent-up stress and tension. Hence, the elderly people are advised to follow some sort of exercise within their capacity and constraints to get relieved from the stressors.
- **Eat a Healthy Diet.** The organs, systems and the body as a whole get stressed if it is not getting the right amount of vitamins and minerals that it needs. Well-nourished bodies are better prepared to cope with stress, so be mindful of the eating practice. As the old age is prone to frequent weakens of bones and nerves it is essential to maintain a healthy and balanced diet according to the necessity of the body, hence, it is advisable to have proper diet by taking the advice of the specialist in the field.
- **Keep Your Sense of Humour.** This includes the ability to laugh by self and make others to laugh, which is the best medicine to overcome stress. The act of laughing helps the body fight stress in a number of ways. Humour

gets the brain thinking and working in a different way - it distracts one from having a stressed mindset. Distraction is a simple effective de-stressor - it takes the thoughts away from the stress, and thereby diffuses the stressful feelings.

- **Focus on the positive. Positive attitude helps a lot to reduce stress and its consequences.** When stress makes one to be depressed, take a moment to reflect on all the things you appreciate in your life, including the positive qualities and gifts. This simple strategy can help the things in perspective.
- **Express the feelings instead of bottling them up.** If something or someone is bothering, try to communicate the feelings to the ones who really care and take concern in an open and respectful way. If this will be the practice, it will reduce the stressful situation to a large extent.
- **Avoid the people who give stress** - If someone consistently causes stress in the life and gives continuous trouble, the better way is to set aside these people from the relationship. Further, it is better to limit the amount of time you spend with that person or end the relationship entirely.
- **Social Support**: The elderly people need and benefit from social support in many ways, which is the better strategy to reduce the stress. Participation of various social organizations and service centres will help the persons to engage fully on different aspects which will automatically work as a great stress reliever.

REFERENCES

Barbara, A. Butrica, Joshua H. Goldwyn and Richard W. Johnson, 2005. "Understanding Expenditure Patterns in Retirement" Center for Retirement Research at Boston College, Working Paper.

Borsch, Axel and Supan, 2004. "Global Ageing; Issues, Answers, More Questions" Michigan Retirement Research Centre, University of Michigan

Gupta, S.P., *Statistical Methods*, S,Chand & Co., New Delhi, 2000

Hagihara. A, Tarunik, Nobutomo. K (2000) *Work stressors, drinking with colleagues after work, and job satisfaction among white-collar workers in Japan.* Department of Health Service Management and Policy, Japan April 35(3), 737-356.

Healthy People 2000, U.S. Department of Health and Human Services.

http://anxietyreliefstress.com/.

http://EzineArticles.com/?expert=Alan_Kelly

http://EzineArticles.com/?expert=Jennifer_A._Johnson

Lusardi, Annamaria, 2005. "Financial Literacy and Planning: Implications for Retirement Well-being" Wharton School, University of Pennsylvania.

"Prevention of Work-Related Psychological Disorders": A National Strategy Proposed by the National Institute for Occupational Safety and Health (NIOSH), *American Psychologist*, Vol. 45, No. 10, October 1990.

Soest, Arthur Van, 2006. "Savings, Portfolio Choice, and Retirement Expectations" Michigan Retirement Research Centre, University of Michigan.

Challenges of Ageing in Urban Context and Possible Social Work Interventions

— A.P. Senthil Kumar

ABSTRACT

This chapter addresses the need for a comprehensive study of the specific problems of senior citizens living in the paid and unpaid homes in Coimbatore. Today both developed and under developed countries are facing the problems of ageing population. Offspring are giving too much pressure towards their elders during the old age period. Hence the challenges of aging results in difference of opinion and attitude between the generations. It needs the right support and intervention. Generally elderly people are neglected and abused. There is a need to explore their circumstances so that their relatives, community members, service providers and the government can design appropriate services for them. Children are migrating to the cities in search of employment, so care of the elderly fall on fewer adult children. Further urbanization and western cultural invasion leads to changes in families and community relationship. Lack of support and understanding lead to maltreatment of the elderly by their own kith and kin. Elder abuse means any conduct or behaviour which causes physical, psychological or financial harm to an older person. Elder abuse includes physical abuse, emotional abuse, sexual abuse, financial abuse, violation of human rights and systemic abuse. Older people are not considered and respected for their knowledge and experiences. The main aim of the study was to assess the socio-economic conditions of the elderly people, level of anxiety and depression of the respondents. This study describes the attributes related to the challenges with the help of descriptive research design. The data was collected through research questionnaire. The researcher randomly selected 60 senior citizens from both paid and unpaid homes in Coimbatore city. Findings of this study reveal that majority of the women are in old age homes than the men (74 per cent). Majority of the elders are in poor socio-economic status (65.5 per cent), most of the elders level of Anxiety (93 per cent) and depression (60 per cent) was in high level.

Key words: *Challenges, Anxiety, Depression, Socio-economic conditions, senior citizens, urbanization and migration etc.*

Introduction

Indian society had traditional informal support systems such as joint family, kin and community. Due to modernization and globalization, the capacity of the traditional informal supports systems slowly weakening and is not in a position to fulfil even the basic needs of the elderly.

According to the U.N. , the world's population now stands at 6.3 billion and will reach 9.3 billion by mid-century. People aged 60 or more are projected to increase from 629 million now to nearly 2 billion by 2050. Furthermore, the elderly population itself is aging. The 80-plus age group makes up the population to increase from 12 per cent to 19 per cent by 2050. This greying of the world is a natural result of falling fertility rates and rising life expectancy.

The powerful combination of globalization, urbanization, cultural thrift and employment crisis of the children made them to keep away from their elders knowledge and experience sharing process.

Despite the belief that children are the security of the aged , institutions for the aged are ,mushrooming since 1990s. In 2001 India had more than 5000 old age homes catering to the needs of poor, widows, destitute and elderly people. Realizing the challenges of the elderly, present study was undertaken to study the functioning of the selected paid home and unpaid homes.

Challenges of Aging: In our society older people are usually cared for in their homes, but because of the changing family structure the elderly parents are left alone in their homes. Their children are moving to the cities for employment. Care of the elderly falls on fewer adult children and urbanisation and migration contribute to the change - taking place in families and community relationships (Gorman 2000). Some of the children taking care of their elderly parents lack support and understanding of the needs of their elderly parents and this may lead to the maltreatment of the elderly.

Elder abuse is a form of family violence (Fawcett, *et al.*, 1996). Family violence usually happens behind closed doors, where an outsider cannot see what is happening. When we talk about domestic violence there is usually a cycle of violence. Social learning theory maintains that violence is learned within the family for example if a child has observed that in his/her family physical abuse and emotional abuse were strategies used to solve problems of stressful situation, they may do the same when they are faced with problems in the care of their parents (Wiehe 1998).

Since there is little consensus on the term elder abuse, for this paper the term elder abuse means any conduct or behaviour which cause physical, psychological or financial harm to an older person (Aged Persons Act, 1967). Elder abuse includes, physical abuse, emotional abuse, sexual abuse, financial abuse, violation of human rights and systemic abuse (Field 1996, Keikelame and Ferreira 2000, Van Dokkum 1996, Fawcett, Featherstone, Hearn and Toft 1996, Wil, Joubert and Lindgren 2001). Van der Geese (1997) in Ghana found that older people are no longer respected and consulted for their knowledge and experiences. He also believed that older people know better than children so they should be respected. The adult children should not respect their own families alone but the whole community and should listen and not talk back (Moller and Sotshongaye: 1999).

Older people are involved in informal education and they transmit customs, traditions, beliefs and convictions from one generation to another within and outside the family circle (Dubazana, 1985). Older people are the guardians of African social values and play a key role in maintaining culture and tradition (Randel, German and Ewing 1999).

Objectives: The researcher conducted this research to increase the percentage of awareness on the catering needs of the elderly people in our society. However, in the light of the limited work available in the Indian context on paid and unpaid old age home research studies, the present study were conducted with the objectives:

1. To study the socio-economic conditions of the elderly people.
2. To assess the Anxiety and depression level of the respondents.
3. To provide the social work intervention to overcome the menace of the elderly people.

Methodology: The study was conducted at two old age homes in Coimbatore city, during 2008-2009. In this study the researcher used descriptive research design. The major purpose of descriptive research design is description of the state of affairs as they exist at the time of the study. The inclusive criterion for this study is 60-80 years of age. Terminally ill patients, more than 80 years have been excluded. Universe of the study was 60-80 years elderly people who were staying in two old age homes during the period of 2008-2009. The researcher used disproportionate random sampling to select 60 respondents from 300. A self-structured questionnaire was prepared to collect the back ground information of the challenges of the elderly people. Most of the sample was female because female admission ratio was high during that time.

Both English and Tamil versions of this form were made available. It contained questions regarding demographic factors, Anxiety and depression. Taylor's (1998) inventory to measure the anxiety level of the elderly. Beck's Depression inventory II (BDI II -1996) is especially designed for depression of geriatric people.

Limitations of the tools: Taylor's (1998) anxiety measurement inventory is applicable only to the 60-80 years of elderly people. Beck's Depression inventory II (BDI II - 1996) is especially designed for depression of geriatric people it is limited to measure only the increasing stress level among the age of above 40 years.

Results and Discussion: As far as the personal profile of the respondents is concerned, majority of them (66.7 per cent) were in the female category. The reasons for that were, life expectancy of the women are more than the male, some of them lost their better half and some were separated from their spouse. In the case of religion, nearly half of the respondents were Hindus. Majority of the respondents had completed their high school education. Nearly two third (50.0 per cent) of their respondents had completed pre-degree and graduation. More than half (57.5 per cent) of them had two children. Half of (50.0 per cent) of the respondents were in the age group of 60-70 years. One fourth (15.o per cent) of the respondents were the pensioners.

Anxiety status of the elderly people: The state of feeling nervous and worries that leads to the state of fear and frustration. Family commitments, expectations and their wards' financial support, lack of love and affection lead to the conflict and finally made them to face depression . The research study shows the following:

Anxiety level	Frequency	percentage
Very high	56	93.33
Low and medium	4	6. 67

It was understood that majority of the respondents (93.33 per cent) experienced very high anxiety.

The study revealed that the reasons for their anxiety level may be due to lack of ability to cope with illness, expectation about self, expectation about others, aversion for responsibility and fear about the future.

Stressors of elderly people: Children's pressure, strain, anxiety, tension, and worries caused the depression state in their way of life, lack of love and affection, illness, psychological imbalance, failure to get remedy etc.

The study shows:

Anxiety level	Frequency	percentage
Very high	36	60.00
Low and medium	24	40.00

It was found that majority of the respondents (60.00 per cent) had experienced high stress; 40.00 per cent experienced low and medium level of stress. The study revealed that most of the elderly people's stress is due to loneliness, isolated from the family and failure to understand the relationship with their wards. Continual psychological harassment by the children and misunderstanding between the daughter-in-law or son-in-law made them to worry about their inability in this world. This leads them to a high risk stress category

Anxiety: There is significant association between Age and Anxiety experienced by the respondents. They are negatively correlated. As the Age increases, the respondents will not be able to do everything like before 60 years. They themselves were convinced and experienced less anxiety.

There is a significant association between education and Anxiety. They are positively correlated. As the educational qualification increases, the respondents will have more anxiety. It is because of their occupational status acquired based on their educational status in their previous years made them to compare the current situation and experienced more anxiety. There is no significant association between income and anxiety of the elderly people. This means the income of the respondents had no influence on anxiety.

Depression: The study revealed that there is a positive correlation was witnessed among the income, educational qualifications of the respondents. Even though some of the respondent's income is high, the respondents felt and raised a question why I am in the home. This insight made them to under go depression. As though they are having educational qualification, the respondent's experiences depression based upon their current conditions not providing any relief based on their qualifications. But the study revealed that Age and depression was negatively correlated. As the age of the respondents increase, he will not be able to provide care to other members in family. They themselves have been convinced and experienced depression.

Intervention Strategies

Micro intervention: At micro level the following strategies should be implemented to empower the elderly in urban context by applying the social case work, social group work and community organization. First apply the social case work among older persons and make them to be self-reliant and empower them to solve their problems themselves. Counselling technique would provide ego strengthening mechanism to boost up their mind set up to face the challenges. During the case work the following areas may be covered as follows.

- Older persons in urban areas should be made aware of their human rights.

- They should be educated about available services.
- They should be educated about their health and all infections.

Secondly the social group work is essential to give guidance to the elderly people through the Care home's social workers. It is essential to identify the strength, weakness, opportunities and threads of the elderly. They should be helped to form support groups, so that they can share their own experiences.

Thirdly the Government and the agency people should provide services to the elderly people in the society related to their daily issues like health, social-security and other basic essential commodities through the community mobilization methods. All services should be made accessible and affordable to the older people, for example, health and social services.

Macro-intervention: Older people can be empowered through participatory research, i.e. when they are asked questions about their problems and helped to prioritize the problems and asked them to come up with possible solution to their problems (Randel *et al.,* 1999).

In the Social welfare Administration, social work methods department officials, social workers, politicians and all other professionals coming into contact with the elderly should receive in service-training so that they can know what to do when they deal with the elderly.

Public awareness campaigns should be under taken by social workers, they should educate the school children and the community members about older people so that they can change their attitude as the part of social action. One elder protection unit in all police stations, according to the act.

Conclusion

Admitting, encouraging the elderly people in the home is not a solution in our social institution. Instead of that elderly people skill, knowledge, experiences and their attitude to be diverted to use the potential use of man hours during their retirement life by encouraging them in any type of business, income generating activities and social service based upon their interest and involvement. Idle mind is devil's workshop. So, if they are engaged in some activities during their old age to avoid unnecessary wordy quarrel, lack of understanding, abuse of the old people by their own ward. So, the family, government, Non-Government organization, employees and the society at large must collectively take steps to improve the socio-economic conditions and to reduce the anxiety and stress level by utilizing the elderly people's skill, knowledge and attitude etc.

We the member of family should be facilitator, friend, and soul saver to them. This will really give rebirth to the elderly people.

REFERENCES

Census of India (1991). *Registrar General and Census Commissioner. India*: Personal Communication Aug.1992.

Department of Health (1999). *Development of natural strategy on elder abuse. Working Document.* Pretoria: Government Printers.

Dubazana H.J.B. (1985). *The elderly and social change in Traditional Zulu Society* : A Study of KwaZulu, South Africa.

Fawcett, B. Featherstone, B Hearn, J & Toft, C. (1996). *Violence and gender relations: Theories and interventions*. Sage Publishers.

Field, A.M. (1997). Discussion *Paper: Financial Exploitation of elder people in their homes.* NSW Advisory Committee on abuse of older people. Sydney.

Gorman, M. (2000). *The growing problem of violence against older persons in Africa. Southern African Journal of Gerontology*, 9(2): 33-36.

Keikelame, J. & Ferreira, M. (2000). Elder *abuse in black townships on the Cape Flats. Research Report.* Cape Town: HSRC/UCT Centre for Gerontology.

Moller, V. and Sotshongaye, A (1999). *Ageing and old age in pre-industrial Africa: elderly persons among 19th century, Xhosa speaking peoples. Southern Africa Journal of Gerontology*, 8(2): 18-27.

Mandal, M. The work of NGOS for older persons. *Help age India Research and Development Journal* 1998; 5 : 22-37.

National Policy on older persons(1996*). A report on Elderly people* (Report nos 4-6.) New Delhi: Government of India.

Randel, J German, T and Ewing, D (1999*). The Aging and Development Report: Poverty, Independence and the World's Older People.* London, Earthscan Publications Ltd.

Peil, M. (1991). Family Support for the Nigerian Elderly. *Journal of Comparative Family Studies*, 22(1) : 85-100.

Schaie, K.W. and Willis, S.L. (1991). *Adult development and aging.* New York : Harper Collins Publishers.

United Nations (UN). (1990). *The sex and age distribution of Population.* Geneva.

Van Dokkum N. (1997). *A durable power of attorney for the older South African. Southern African Journal of Gerontology*, 6(1) :17-20.

Van der Geest S (1997). *Between respect and reciprocity : managing old age in rural Ghana. . Southern African Journal of Gerontology*, 6(2): 20-25.

Wiehe, R. V. (1998). *Understanding family violence.* U.S.A : Sage publishers.

Wil, B. Joubert, J. & Lindgren, P. (2001). *Hear Help Heal. A joint report by the South African Council for the Aged (SACA), Halt Elderly Abuse Line (HEAL), and the Medical Research Council (MRC). Cape Town.*

Republic of South Africa (1996). *The Constitution of the Republic of South Africa. Constitutional Assembly*: Cape Town.

Social Networking and Strategic Alliance for Prevention of Elder Abuse

A Policy Framework for India

— Tribhuvan Nath
— Bushara Bano

ABSTRACT

Elder abuse is a growing social problem in India. Elderly people are likely to face both neglect and violence. Researches have reported that the problem of elder abuse is linked to rapid transition in demographics, urbanization, globalization, westernization and modernization which disrupts traditional family system and affects social fabrics and economic pattern. The traditional functions of the family to care and respect older family members are gradually decreasing due to disintegration of the traditional joint family system and loss of value based Indian culture which is respectful and supportive of elders. The changing economic pattern strain households with scarce resources, resulting in isolation and abuse against older members who are perceived as a family burden. Current statistics indicate that with increasing nation's elderly population (currently almost 8% of the total population) growing numbers of elder abuse cases are being reported than in past years. It has brought an increase in the rage and intensity of the elder's problems and needs. Therefore, there is an increased need for care and social support to elderly that is urgently required.

This study presents an effective policy framework based on two different case studies conducted in different social setting which forms alliances and social networking of important institutions like health departments, police departments, NGOs, community organizations and legal institutions in order to prevent elder abuse and livelihood support to older people for their better quality of life.

Introduction

The developing nations like India is confronting the issues of ageing that must be addressed through effective strategies and policy response (Chattopadhyay, 2004; Jamuna, 2003). Changing demographics, urbanization, industrialization, westernization, modernization, migration, recession and consequent economic hardship, break up of joint family, and rise of dual-career families have affected the social fabric and economic pattern of households which isolates older persons and make them more vulnerable to abuse (Giele, 1982 and Penhale, 1997). The demographic trends indicates that India's ageing population, defined as 60 years and above, had accelerated in the last century and will continue in future. According to census, the ageing population in the country shot up from 12 million in 1901, to 19 million in 1951 and 77 million in 2001. The demographic transition is attributed to the decreasing fertility and mortality rates due to the availability of better health care services. Currently the older population account for almost 8 percent of the total population, projected to be 142 million in 2020 and 301 million in 2051, the issue of elder abuse[1] and neglect can no longer be ignored.

The outcomes of HelpAge India study on elder abuse which were conducted across eight cities (Delhi, Mumbai, Ahmedabad, Kolkata, Bhopal, Chennai, Patna and Hyderabad) in India, indicates that about 20 percent of the elderly did not know what constitutes abuse. Among those who were aware, more than one third felt elder abuse constitutes: from feeling disrespected due to verbal abuse, economic abuse, neglect, emotional abuse and physical abuse. The elderly females are more abused than males (Dudley, 1983). The personal losses associated with elderly abuse can be devastating and include the loss of independence, homes, life savings, health, dignity, and security. Researches have reported that most of the abused elderly people belonging to poor families (mostly of below poverty line, BPL) of rural areas and living in vulnerable situation without adequate food, clothing, or shelter and they are perceived as burdens to their families. Further, according to NSS 52nd round data results, around 63 percent of the elderly in India are illiterates, and only 44 percent of the elderly men and 24 percent of the elderly women are currently economically active, while the majority are not economically active and dependent on other. Elderly people experience a stage of transition from independence to interdependence, then to total dependence, which produces a crises and tension for all generations (Steinmetz, 1988).

Ageing is mainly associated with social isolation, lack of current earnings, poverty, apparent reduction in family support, inadequate housing, impairment of cognitive functioning, poor health status and illness, widowhood, bereavement, and limited options for living arrangement and dependency towards end of life (Bennett *et al.*, 1993; Wolf, 1997; McCreadie, 2003). All these problems have an impact on the well-being and quality of life in old age. However, the well-being of old people may also be affected by their own personality problems. If the person has not created quality of social networks and maintains good relationship with his or her family members throughout life, then it becomes difficult to improve relationships in later period. The regular interaction, linkages and meaningful relationships with individuals, institutions and community lead to strengthen the social networks that plays important role in crises situations like old age. To deal with the ageing issues, strategic alliance between institutions of the same interest is emerging as an integrated social service delivery mechanism. The alliances are collaborative partnership between government, non-government and community organizations to fighting against elder abuse through their own experiences and expertise. Across the globe such collaborative practices are already practicing and have gain success to deal with ageing issues. This mechanism can be adopted in Indian context as a strategic policy response to ageing issues.

Since the Independence of India, health program and policies have been focusing on issues like population stabilization, maternal and child health, and disease control. However, issues of ageing in India gives a prelude to a new set of medical, social, and economic problems that could arise if a timely initiative in this direction is not taken by the policy makers. There is an urgent need to rethink of social security policy and strategies for bringing about an improvement in quality of life of the older people.

This chapter presents theoretical perspective of social networking and success story of strategic alliances in dealing with ageing issues. Based on the theoretical perspective, literature survey and lesson from the case study this study presents an elderly policy framework for India.

Objectives and Methodology: The major objective of the present study is to design an elderly policy framework for India by identifying the major areas of intervention and types of intervention needed. The specific objectives of the study are as following:

- To design the conceptual framework of social networking
- To identify major areas of intervention for effective elderly policy
- To suggest types of intervention in each identified area
- To suggest strategy as an effective policy response for interventions in the identified areas

As of the study methodology concerned, a detailed literature review on the various aspects of elderly abuse and on existing elderly policies in the country was conducted. The secondary data on elders' opinion on areas of Govt. intervention for elderly care is used from the study conducted by Chattopadhya (2004). This paper also adopted case study methodology to discuss the strategic policy response and approach to deal with the ageing issues.

Social Networking: A Conceptual Framework

Preparedness from childhood is the best way to securing the older life. The quality of relationship of individuals with family members and resilient neighbourhoods and communities provides the social security throughout life. There are several financial insurance mechanisms are available in forms of pension and insurance that offer better way to financial security for elderly life. Social networking is the traditionally and culturally suitable mechanism to secure and protect the elder people.

Social networking is the web of social relations. Social networks, for the purpose of study, will include individuals and multiple linkage groups across the ecological framework (Figure 23.1). An ecological framework is constructed with four levels: individuals, relationship, community and society. The individual's quality of relationship at all levels of the wider ecological framework is an important criteria to asses the strength and length of social networks created by individual to get help and to support the network people in crises situations like old age. Social networks play important role in providing social security, financial security and emotional security not only in adverse situations of the old age but also entire period of life cycle. A good interaction between family members is not guarantee for full proof social security, without involving the other actors involved in providing social protection and services. The responsibility for dependency must be wider across the ecological framework of the social networks in order to ensure not only social security but also financial and emotional security. The social networks expanded across the ecological framework have the huge potential to influence and change the overall elderly support system for positive outcomes of individuals, institutions, community and society for improved quality of life of elder people.

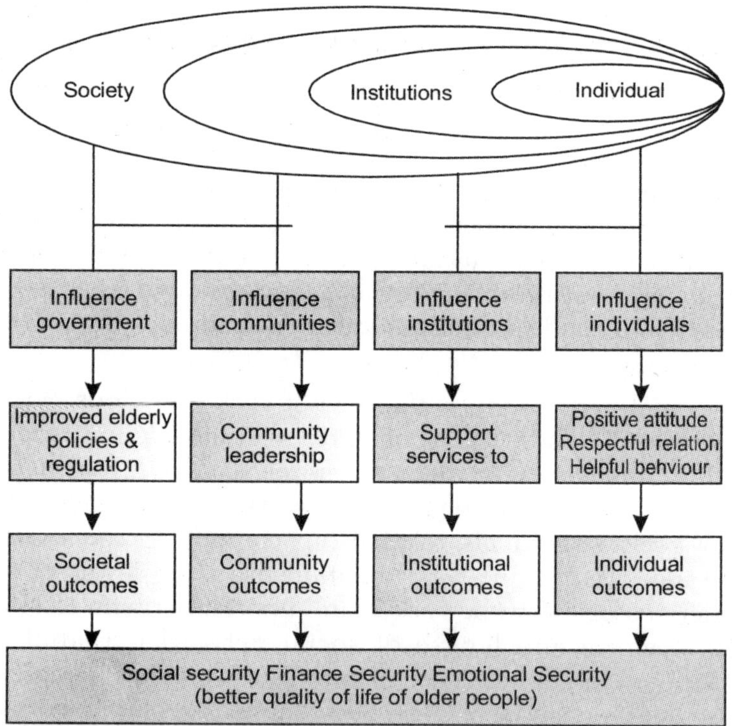

Fig. 23.1 : The Conceptual Framework: Ecological Framework, Social Networks and Outcomes

Forming strategic alliances with other businesses for profit is very common in corporate sector. However, this arrangement is also increasingly practiced in non-profit and social sector as an effective social service delivery mechanism that coordinates services. The social institutions (that delivers social services) in the country are generally fragmented and hence inefficient is delivering the social services. There is need of integrated service delivery mechanism to effectively deliver the social services and outreach. There are several cases practicing in different social setting that have shown that strategic alliance between institutions of same interest is very effective in delivering the social services and outreach.

The Alliance for the Prevention of Elder Abuse: Western Australia (APEA: WA) is an alliance of Western Australian organisations including Government departments which have an interest in matters relevant to older people and support/ assist older people who are experiencing elder abuse (Figure 2). The alliance promotes a whole-of-government policy framework that values older people and supports the rights of older people. The goals of APEA:WA are:

- To raise community knowledge and understanding of elder abuse;
- To provide policy advice on elder abuse;
- To expand the breadth and quality of knowledge of elder abuse;

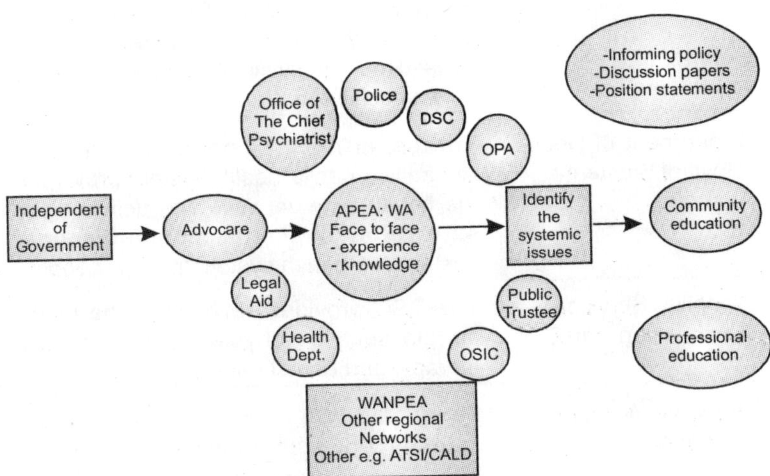

Fig. 23.2 : APEA: WA partners and delivery of community and social services

- To support provision of adequate elder abuse prevention and protection services; and
- To promote professional education and training in elder abuse issues.

Table 23.1 describes the APEA: WA alliance partners and their roles and responsibilities. Table clearly indicates that multidisciplinary organizations/institutions of same interest are involved in different capacities and approach to deliver social services and advocacy to older people and educate community. This APEA is very successful in delivering the social services, advocacy, protecting right and empowerment of older people.

Table 23.1: Alliances partners and their roles and responsibilities

Organizations	Roles and Responsibilities
1	2
Advocare	Advocare is an independent advocacy agency which advocates and protects the rights of older people. The abused older people or those who are at risk of being abused may directly/indirectly call Advocare on a specific number.
Department of Health (Govt. of Western Australia)	The department of health is Western Australia's public health system providing the health care services and delivering a safe, high quality, accountable and sustainable health system to older people.
Disability Services Commission (DSC)	The DSC provides services to the older people such as physiotherapy, speech therapy, and dental care etc.
Legal Aid Western Australia	Legal Aid Western Australia is an independent statutory body funded by both the Commonwealth and State governments. It provides information, advice and other legal help to older people.

1	2
Office for Seniors Interests and Volunteering (OSIV)	OSIV aims to enhance the lifestyles of seniors by promoting positive ageing and encouraging the community to plan for its ageing population.
Office of the Chief Psychiatrist (Govt. of WA, Dept. of Health)	The Office Chief Psychiatrist has independent responsibilities for the medical care and welfare of older people, and the monitoring of standards of psychiatric care.
Office of the Public Advocate (OPA)	The Office of the *Public Advocate* works to promote and protect the human rights older people with decision making disabilities. It also provides advocacy and educate community.
Public Trustee	Public Trustee is a Government Business Enterprise that provide services on personal estate planning services, investment services, taxation, real estate management, public education and preparation.
WA Police	The WA Police provides home based security and safety to older people under the specific Home and Community Care Program (HACC).

Policy Framework to Prevention of Elderly Abuse: As the ageing issues differ from those of the general population, the elderly policies require to address these issues differently. The United Nations Principles address the independence, participation, care, self-fulfilment and dignity of older persons as an ensured priority. Well-being of older persons has been mandated in the Constitution of India. Article 41 of the Directive Principles of State Policy in the Indian Constitution specifies that the State shall, within the limits of economic capacity, provide for assistance to the elderly. Elder people's social security has been made the concurrent responsibility of the Central and State Governments. Section 125 of the

Criminal Procedure Code, 1973, specifies the rights of parents without any means for maintenance to be supported by their children having sufficient means. Over the years, the government has launched various schemes and policies for the welfare of older persons. The National Policy for Older Persons was launched in 1999 to promote the healthcare, shelter and welfare of senior citizens in India. In the end of year 2007 Indian parliament has passed a bill known as Maintenance of parents and Senior citizens Act that seeks to make it a legal obligation for children and heirs to provide maintenance to senior citizens. However, ageing population in the country is reflected in rising demand for social welfare and long-term care of the elderly. As more people live longer, retirement, pensions, and other social benefits tend to be extended over longer periods of time.

Chattopadhya (2004), based on survey of 275 retired male pensioners' residing in Mumbai resulted that 71 percent of the retirees do think that there is a need for state intervention to enhance the quality of life of aged people in general and pensioners in particular. Table 23.2 clearly indicates that of those who feel that government intervention is the need of the hour to tackle the problems of the elderly, 63 per cent have demanded improvement in the medical and health care facilities, followed by welfare aspects, financial security and housing.

Table 23.2: Opinion on areas of Government Intervention

Areas of intervention	Opinion (%)
Medical/health	63.2
Economic	55.9
Transport	29.1
Housing	41.1
Justice and law	6.8
Culture/recreation	20.9
Welfare	58.2

Source: Chattopadhyay, 2004.

Table 23.2 clearly indicates about the major areas of interventions needed to policy support on elderly. However, there are numerous programs for the elderly launched by government but they are malfunctioning and fail to address the demand of older people. There is an urgent need to reform the elderly policies and programmes in consideration to need and demand of older people. In consideration to findings of Table 23.2, Table 23.3 presents the elderly policy framework for the areas of intervention along with type of intervention in each particular area. The major areas of intervention identified for the elderly, composed of health services, medical services, pension programs, housing, long-term care, welfare for elderly people, and advocacy and education.

Table 23.3: Elderly Policy Framework for the Major Areas of Intervention and Types of Intervention

Areas of Intervention	Types of Interventions
1	2
Health	Health education
	Health counselling
	Provision for regular medical check-up
	Opening of geriatric ward in government hospitals
	Improvement in the service of government health scheme
Medical Services	Health service system for the elderly
	Provision of costly medicine at a subsidised rate
	Compulsory medical insurance
Pension	Old-age pension for destitute elderly
	Old-age pension for those 60 and above
	Increase pension/indexing pension with inflation
	Tax free pension

1	2
Housing	Providing pension on time
	Provision of old-age home
	Old-age ashrams
	Improving quality of service of old-age homes
	Compulsory accommodation of aged parents
Long-term Care	In-home services
	Expanding home care services
	Rehabilitative medical care
	Special nursing home for the elderly
	Transportation facilities
	Provision of allowance for people with specialdisabilities
Welfare for Elderly People	Expanding employment opportunities
	Livelihood support measures
	Abuse help line services
	Welfare center for the elderly
Advocacy & Education	Information and community education
	Training to health care professionals
	Free advocacy to older people

Governments alone can not take care of all the needs of the older population. The private sector consisting of the Voluntary Agencies and community organizations including the family must have to play an important role in this regard. The Non-Governmental Organizations (NGO) sector constitutes a very important institutional mechanism to provide user friendly, affordable services to take care of the elderly persons. However, this sector in India is playing only a minor role catering only to a rather small segment of the old age population, which is capable of paying for the services rendered.

As an effective intervention strategy, strategic alliances between different government department/institutions which have an interest in matters relevant to older people including NGOs, private sector, voluntary agencies and community organizations may offer better social services delivery mechanism to ageing population.

Conclusion

The demographic transition along with other influencing factors as discussed above has implications at the macro (society and economy) and also at household level. Longer life spans are creating new opportunities but also new risks necessitating a fundamental rethink of social security policy in long-life societies. Social security has been made the concurrent responsibility of the Central and State Governments. The Government of India has expressed its concern in this regard by preparing the National Policy on the Older Persons and Maintenance of parents and Senior citizens Act. However, Governments alone can not take care of all the needs of the older population. To proper deal with the issues of ageing, there is need of proper strategic response and policy support. Preparedness from childhood and social networking is traditionally and culturally appropriate mechanism of social security for latter life. Older people's participation in social networks is a significant component of wellbeing. Social networking can make elderly people to feel valued, a part of a community, and earn the respect for their rich experience and wisdom.

Strategic alliances in social sector have emerged as an integrated social service delivery mechanism to deal with elderly issues. The Alliance for the prevention of elder abuse: Western Australia (APEA: WA) is the live example of the success of the strategic alliances between multidisciplinary organizations/institutions of same interest to deliver social services, advocacy of older people and to educate community. In Indian context, the strategic response to interventions areas of the elderly policy framework can be made through forming strategic alliances between institutions of the same interest including private agencies, NGOs, community organizations, voluntary organizations and Panchayti Raj Institutions (PRIs) in order to effective delivery of social services and protection of older people for their better quality of life.

REFERENCES

Bennett, G. and Kingston P (1993), *Elder abuse, concepts, theories and interventions,* London, Chapman & Hall, 1993.

Chattopadhyay, A. (2004), "Population Policy for the Aged in India", *Economic and Political Weekly, Vol. 39,* No. 43, pp. 4694-4696.

Dudley, A. (1983), "Relationship with male and female elders", *Smith College Studies in Social Work,* Vol. 53, 177¾87.

Giele, J. Z. (1982), "Family and Social Network", pp 40-74 in International Perspective on Ageing: Population and Policy Challenges, Policy Document Studies, No 7, United Nations Fund for Population Activities.

Jamuna D. (2003), "Issues of elder care and elder abuse in the Indian context", *J Aging Soc Policy,* Vol. 15, pp. 125-42.

McCreadie C. (2003), "The nature of elder abuse", In: Amiel S, Heath I, (eds.) *Family Violence in Primary Care,* Oxford University Press, pp.374–379.

Penhale B. and Kingston P. (1997), "Elder abuse, mental health and later life: steps towards an understanding", *Aging and Mental Health*, Viol. 1, pp. 296–304.

Steinmetz, S. K. (1988). *Duty Bound: Elder Abuse and Family Care.* Newbury Park, CA: Sage Publications.

Wolf R.S. (1997), "Elder abuse and neglect: causes and consequences", *Journal of Geriatric Psychiatry*, pp. 30:155–159.

Current Scenario of Networking of Aged Care Organizations in India

– Dr. P. Vyasamoorthy

ABSTRACT

There are many types of organizations connected with senior citizens like: Senior Citizens Associations, Day Care Centres, Walkers Clubs, Resident Welfare Associations, Retirees Associations, Pensioners Associations, NGOs in aged care, Old Age Homes, Pay & Stay Senior facilities, Specialized gated communities, Counselling Centres, Elders Help lines, Women's Self Help Groups, Support groups for dementia or Parkinson's, Geriatric hospitals, nursing homes and palliative care centres etc

The need for and advantages of Inter and intra networking among these various types of organizations can be examined from several points of view, especially from prevention of Elder Abuse and improving the quality of life of aged persons towards a life with dignity & respect.

A description of current scenario obtaining in India in this regard will be provided. This will show how the organizations are networked (or the lack of it) within each type. The need to interlinking all types organizations will be explained and methods of networking discussed.

The description of current scenario will include brief info on INPEA, Aadhar, Aasara, SCAs and federations, NASCAI, efforts of the Planning Commission, newly formed Joint Action Committee, Virtual networks (like sss-global, verdurez) HelpAge, SSS, private NGOs Networks, and Helplines. Providers of services like: Listening services, counselling, Errands, training, Entertainment, etc have a role to play in mitigating the sufferings of old people. Networking of this group, including products and goods suppliers (assistive devices and others) will also be discussed.

Following this, recommendations of what needs to be done to improve the situation – explaining who may do what – will be made.

Introduction

There are many types of organizations connected with senior citizens. For the sake of our convenience we may group them into two broad categories, the first one where senior citizens themselves are constituent members (here senior citizens help themselves) and the second one where the organizations provide some kind of service or sell goods and products (here senior citizens are targets for service). From networking point of view, it would be useful to discuss each type in some detail, to start with. We may look into: the characteristics of each type of seniors related organization; whether any networking among them is available as of now; their strengths and weaknesses etc Thereafter we may discuss inter and intra networking feasibilities, advantages of networking and identify who could take up this responsibly. Throughout the discussions requirements of older persons especially for prevention and mitigation of elder abuse / human rights violation of elders will be kept in mind.

Type 1: Senior Citizen Groups that Serve Themselves

Let us discuss Type 1 of organizations to start with. Table 24.1 lists out the typical organizations involved here.

Table 24.1 : Types of Aged Care Organizations: Type 1: Organizations where seniors them selves are members (Helping themselves)

Fully consisting of SC	Mostly consisting of SC
Senior Citizens Associations	Resident Welfare Associations
Pensioners Associations	Morning walkers associations
Retirees associations	Women's Self Help Groups
Federations & Confederations at State & National level	Bajan groups

Senior Citizens Associations

Characteristics of SCA: Senior citizens voluntarily come together and form associations. Generally it is a localized affair. They may be registered or not. The purpose is to keep members occupied and useful. Periodical meetings, health camps, reading rooms, indoor games, local trips, get together, newsletters, social service activities like health camps, eye camps, etc generally form the agenda. Some SCAs organize computer training. Some offer training in Yoga, pranayama etc. Spiritual discourses are common. Socialization among members such as celebrating birthdays, wedding days, visiting the sick or lonely seniors is normal. Senior Citizens Forum in Secunderabad, serving seniors for the past 15 years, is a noted one.

Role in Elder Abuse: A closely knit group of elders can play useful role in helping victims of Elder abuse. Primary approach practised is visiting the house and counselling the youngsters who are the abusers. Liaising with tribunal for award of justice is another area. Publicizing information about abuse occurrence itself may prevent further deterioration as the abusers are likely to suffer adverse publicity. State level organizations may nominate representatives in the district level tribunals set up for awarding compensation in EA cases under Maintenance and Welfare of Parents and Senior citizens Act 2007.

AP scenario: In Hyderabad alone there are more than 80 SCAs. There are about 350 SCAs in AP. These have come together under two state level federations: FAPSCO - Federation of Andhra Pradesh Senior Citizens Organizations and APSCCON - Andhra Pradesh Senior Citizens Confederation. Government of AP recognizes both. State level Federations have federated into National level confederations. Unfortunately more than six or seven organizations claim to be working at national level. All India Senior Citizens Confederation, Respect Age International, Indian Federation for Aging, Indian association of Retired Persons, Karnataka State Federation of Senior Citizens are such top level claimants. There is no consensus amongst them as to who is the leader.

All India Senior Citizens' Confederation : Let us look at **All India Senior Citizens' Confederation**, the largest of such National level federation, (http://www.aisccon.org) in some detail. It was established in 2001 and has member associations in 14 states and 2 UTs representing senior citizen strength of 3 lakhs. Considering that India has 900 Lakhs of senior citizens, this representation is far too insignificant. However, this is the largest! The annual seminar held in various cities without any break serves as a useful event for get together of SCAs. The monthly newsletter - AISCCON News - is available in print as well as online. Recently it moved into its own building in Navi Mumbai.

Networking of SCAs: Effective networking and strengthening membership in all states is extremely important to become heard, leave alone EA cause. For example just one association Kerala run by Master Balan has 1 lakh members but it is not yet a member of AISCCON. Recently for the past two years, there have been attempts to bring all leading national level bodies under one umbrella. Gangadhran of Heritage succeeded to some extent in forming NASCAI (National Alliance for Senior Citizens Associations in India). HelpAge India is also trying to bring together, claiming support of several hundred Vruddha Sanghas they have helped forming in rural India. The National Policy on Older Persons (NPOP) specifically provides for promotion of a National Association of Older Persons and the Planning Commission has included this as a notable point in the implementation of 11th Five-year Plan.

At last they are coming together: Interestingly, some kind of unity seems to be cropping up due mounting social pressure. Frustrated over the gross negligence and abject abuse of seniors community by the State and Central governments for the past several decades, several state level and national level associations have come together voluntarily (as many as 27) to observe a "Senior Citizens National Protest Day on 16th August 2010". The member associations showing support is given in the Appendix 1.

Pensioners Associations: Pensioners Associations essentially cater to the requirements of people retiring from government service - state and central - who constitute about 10% of entire Senior citizen community. There are a very large number of pensioners associations very wide and varied in constitution, coverage and activity. There are such associations for railways, Telephones, individual banks, CSIR, ICAR, RBI, LIC etc. There even a tiny one for retired teachers from Central schools. Their activity is mostly limited to helping members with difficulties in getting pension, fixation, payment, continuation etc. It is only very recently that they have started looking at themselves as senior citizens with a large number of problems other than pension. They are seeking entry into SCAs group for mutual benefit. Bharat Pensioners Samaj and Rtired Railway Employees Association (http://www.rrewa.org) are large ones worth mentioning.

The chief advantage of Pensioners association is that they a well knit group with formal and informal networking amongst all of them. As they collect a large sum of money by way of membership and members are good many they have financial resources to have their own buildings everywhere!

Ea is a not specific issue peculiar to pensioners – they are relatively well off financially. They join associations for camaraderie and social networking.

Retirees Associations This type of association caters to all types of retirees and all members have retired from active service. Examples are CSIR retired officers association, ICAR retired officers association. Membership is likely to grow continuously. The binding factor is the multicity organization for which they worked. In a way there are in a shell of their own, restricting reach to a smaller group. I am not aware of any networking amongst these, the very nature of the bodies being discretely tied down to former employer. Any networking aimed at senior citizens as a whole should take this group into its fold.

Peripheral Organizations: Walkers Associations, Bajan Groups, Resident Welfare Associations, Woman's' Self Help Groups etc are other groups that contain a good number of old people. They need to be roped in as partners in any worthwhile network for aged people. At present they are spread far and wide with no unification.

Walkers International (http://walkersinternational.in), established in 1986 is a well networked organization with about 580 members (walkers clubs) as of date; Most of the members are from India, though the name is International. A very large number of activities are taken up towards welfare of the society/community by walkers clubs. The organizational structure is similar to Lions Clubs or Rotary clubs with districts headed by district presidents. It has its headquarters in Visakapatnam. A newsletter, published regularly every month, gives updated info. The website is updated promptly and periodically.

There is a need for including walkers club into seniors' Network. As most walkers are members in more than one association, bringing up synergy by inter-association contacts is easy. This already happening in Visakapatnam – HQ; A good number of walkers / senior citizens are taking active part in a call by AISCCON/APSCCON for observing a protest day. Formal unification is not far away.

Walkers chat a lot during their morning walk. This is useful group for handling EA situations. Experience sharing, locating help, house visits etc are possible.

Bajan groups and Women's Self Help Groups: As an example of integration, I may cite that Society for Serving Seniors conducts entertainment programs in Old Age Homes in and around Hyderabad and the help of Bajan groups are utilized. As all persons from different groups are senior citizens, mixing and interaction among themselves is beneficial. Bajan groups are highly localized and linking them upwards may not be useful.

Type 2: Groups that serve Senior Citizens

Let us now discuss organizations of Type 2 where they serve senior citizens community as a whole.

Organizations that serve seniors community

(In the table below * bodies have no direct impact on EA)

Service / Goods / products Providers to SC
Helplines
Counselling Centres / Legal Aid Centres
Dementia / Alzheimer's Care Centres
Terminal care wings of hospitals / Nursing Homes and Palliative care Units
Old Age Homes free and paid
Builders of (Gated) retirement communities*
Suppliers of Assistive devices*
Publishers / portals/ websites / newsletters*
Errand service, Listening service etc
Day Care Centres
Aged Care NGOs / VOs
Providers of Bedside assistants and their trainers

Helplines: We shall limit the discussion to helplines set up exclusively for senior citizens. Most helplines allow customers to reach them over phone lines and answer queries raised by them. The purpose of such helplines could be to:

- Provide information say on OAH, AED, Location of some office etc
- Help personal relationship issues, Elder abuse; referrals.
- Help in cases of abandonment; legal problems; emergency health or medical care
- Help in personal work: payments, purchases of medicines, errands

They may be run by private NGOs or by the government. The languages in which queries are answered matters. Most helplines accept the local language and English as the medium of communication. If the number of calls per day is far too many then the helpline may go for multiple lines. They usually depend upon standard online databases, printed directories and local readily available experts. They are manned by trained staffs who are patient listeners. They are trained in human psychology, the data sets they would be handling, computer usage etc. Almost always, all the phone based helpline services are free. Vyasamoorthy has discussed details of as many as twenty helplines for older persons in various cities in India. According to him, there are 7 helplines in Hyderabad, 5 in Mumbai, 3 in Ahmadabad, 3 in Delhi, 2 each in Pune and Bangalore. Cities like Allahabad, Calcutta, Chandigarh, Gulbarga, Mangalore, and Coimbatore have one Helpline each. Many helplines have the co-operation and blessings of local Police department.

Aasara helpline in Hyderabad is managed by HelpAge for GHMC, Hyderabad. They have close interaction with some 150 SCAs and 50 day Care centers. About a thousand volunteers offer free service. Right from routine queries about old age homes to emergencies such as snake entry into the house are handled. Issue of ID cards is a major activity. Regular monthly meetings are help. It has gained a reputation for dependability within a short time.

There is no formal networking among helplines. However there is good amount of interaction between the Aasara helpline (Hyderabad) and the SCAs and other organizations. If all helplines are interlinked then a number of benefits will be available: They can reach out to more customers; they can benefit by other's experience; they can pool and create a common database of Questions and answers that will minimize wastage of time and efforts.

Karmayog Mumbai is right now (June 2010) updating its directory of Support groups and Helplines. If the numbers are large then some coalescence may be possible.

Counselling Centres and Legal Aid Centres: Almost every big city has counselling centres of many sorts – psychological, suicide prevention, family relationships, harassment by husbands, dowry harassments etc. Those devoted to Elders exclusively are relatively rare. In Hyderabad there are two: one run by the support of Dr Reddys Lab called Roshni and another one organized by Satya Sai Devotees. They will benefit by collaborating with SCAs and others in widening their reach. Again as the activity is localized upward networking, except for annual get together and seminars at national or state level, may not be useful.

Alzheimer's and Dementia Care Centres: The country is well organized as far as patients of Alzheimer's disease and dementia is concerned, thanks to establishment of Alzheimer's and Related Disorders Society of India in Kerala in 1992. ARDSI has many branches in Kerala itself: Kozhikode, Calicut, Trissur, Trivandrum, Kottayam, and Pattanamthotitta. The Head quarter is in Kannakulam. Branches outside Kerala are in Chennai, Mumbai, Coimbatore, Bengaluru, Kolkata, Delhi, Goa and Hyderabad. The society offers A-Z services including Day Care Centers, Memory Clinics, Training for Care Givers, and Training in geriatrics relating to Dementia patients,

Counselling etc. The annual conferences and World Alzheimer's Day (21 Sep every year) are occasions where members get to meet and network. Chapters in Hyderabad, Kolkata and Mumbai are very active. The Hyderabad Chapter has a virtual network through a Google group to exchange information. Regular monthly meetings for caregivers and running a "weekly once activity cèntre" are other activities.

MOSJE, GOI has taken special notice of the need for supporting Alzheimer's related activity.

While networking within ARDSI community is excellent, collaborating with other senior citizens groups, both horizontally and vertically, will be very useful and essential. This can be supported / promoted by Ministry of Health and Family welfare.

As per World Alzheimer's Report, in India there are about 3 million people with Dementia. The number may go up to 10 million by 2030. This is presently 4% of senior citizens population. Such elderly citizens are most likely to be victims of abuse and neglect. Considering the deadly consequences of this disease for the patients, care givers and families, effective networking on all India basis will lessen the problems. (http://alzheimer.org.in)

Terminal care, Hospices, and Palliative care Units: Patients who are terminally ill are taken care of in hospices or palliative care units. Palliative care consists in caring for patients suffering from pain for a long time. Patients suffering from Cancer, Aids, Cardiac or renal diseases, paralysis and others require palliative care. Any patient suffering from intense pain requiring long term care can benefit from Hospices. The objective of hospices is to improve the quality of life and render living passable. Hospices address all the issues in an integrated way. Where needed, medicines like morphine are given in required doses to reduce pain. Wherever supplemental medical treatment or other interventions like chemotherapy, ration therapy, dialysis etc are indicated, these are provided with the support of nearby hospitals. Counselling is provided to make patient understand and accept the reality. Love, care, company, psychological supports are all given.

Scene in India: The concept itself is relatively new to India. It is believed that even the few centres that have come up in recent years have their origins in the spurt in medical tourism targeting India. Palliative care centres in India are woe fully inadequate as there are only about 55 such centres (August 2009), that too only in major cities. Providing care in hospices requires multi disciplinary skills. Nursing and medical courses make just a passing mention of this service. Indian Association of Palliative Care, Kozhicode, Kerala, Pallium India again in Kerala, Karunashraya in Bangalore provide short term training programs for personnel to be employed in Hospices. Christian Medical College, Vellore offers PG courses in Palliative Medicine supported by its 2000 bedded hospital and a full fledged hospice. Many Old Age Homes who admit sick people also offer quasi (unqualified or unprofessional?) palliative care. If we consider just cancer alone there are nearly one million patients added every year. All major cancel hospitals put together can not handle so many patients. Exclusive hospices are needed.

Networking of such centers among themselves, and across the nation linking with senior citizens groups, with the help of MOSJE and MOHFW will be beneficial. Large NGOs like HelpAge may play a major role here.

Old Age Homes: Old Age Home, both Pay and Stay and Free of charges, are another segment of institutions connected with older people. There are more than 1400 Old Age Homes in India as per latest (2009) directory published by HelpAge India. In AP there are 586 old age homes according FAPSCO Directory published in 2007 but most are defunct - many exist only on paper!.Having to live in an OldAge Home - even in Pay and Stay type - is indeed a curse. People are forced out of circumstances. The conditions are miserable - residents suffer from loneliness, under nutrition, neglect, abuse and exploitation. Institutional abuse is rampant, including financial exploitation, neglect and at times physical too.

In AP, most OldAge Homes have joined a Federation of Elder Homes started two years ago. Dr Koteswar Rao, head of Gold Age chain of senior homes, is the president. This federation is neither active nor effective. I am not aware of similar federations elsewhere. As MWPSCA 2007 has provision for setting up Old Age homes in every district, MOSJE is the best agency to further the cause of bringing all old age homes pan India together. Under its funding and monitoring, some large association like AISCCON or NASCAI may take up this task. Linking all OAH together under one umbrella will pave way for standardization of services, proper categorization similar the stars given to hotels etc. Suitable monitoring mechanisms may also be brought in. ILC, Pune, has enough expertise gathered in this area.

Networking of OAH at the district & state level may be useful from prevention of Elder Abuse also. However vertical or hierarchical networking may not essential from EA point of view. Such a scene is also far away.

Builders of Gated Retirement Communities: People after retirement may decide to buy and move into their own flats or houses built in specialized retirement communities. In such places the building perse has all elders' requirements like: grab bars in bath rooms, anti skid flooring, calling bell for emergencies, common prayer hall, common dining hall, swimming pool, walker's path, services like supply of food from common kitchen, centralized security, library, internet, first aid, transport and so on. Many such facilities are coming up in and around cities.

Saket, Dhyana Prastha, Rajeev Swagruha in Hyderabad, Alliance group in Chennai, LIC housing in Bangalore and Shobhaa Developers, Rakindo Group, Brigade Group, Ashiana Group of Builders, Paranjape Schemes and Riverdale Retirement Resorts elsewhere are some prominent developers concentrating in this sector. Jones Lang LaSalle

Meghraj has made extensive survey in this field. Apparently there is not much scope for these builders coming together among themselves - basically because of a sense of competition. It is also because the field is nascent and just growing. The need for unity surfaces at an advanced stage.

This segment has limited role in Elder abuse except for equipping the building with devices for handling emergencies (fire alarms, theft alarms etc). In Hyderabad the city police offer Omniplis service. Using this facility a lonely single senior can press a bell in emergencies. The police headquarters are directly alerted and help is rushed immediately. Such modern centralized facilities may be provided as a common service for a group flats only by progressive builders.

Suppliers of Assistive Devices: Old age is accompanied by a series of disabilities like loss of hearing, poor vision, difficulty in maintaining balance while walking etc. Assistive devices like a walking stick, spectacles, hearing aids, wheel chairs, magnifying glass etc play a supporting role in maintaining good quality of life. Suppliers of such devices equipments and tools are an integral part of seniors' community. The relationship is comparable to that between a librarian and booksellers, the doctor and medical shops.

This industry is not big as now but has the potential of growing large enough to warrant them getting united. ILC Pune has a directory of manufacturers and suppliers of such Assistive and enabling devices (AED) in India. Ministry of Science and Technology with the help of AIIMS Delhi has set up a website called Old Age Solutions - Portal on technology solutions for the elderly. There is a substantial section on Assistive devices. The Website of Tradeindia (http://www.tradeindia.com/) is a good source for locating new suppliers.

Networking of this trade group with other senior citizens organizations will be useful in certain ways. Suppliers can reach their customers more easily and expand their business. They can be of value in funding and donating for social activities connected with aged people. Apart from this as already indicated this group has no direct bearing in mitigating EA.

Publishers, Portals, websites and Newsletters: The next group we may consider is the traditional and technological Information disseminating agencies. These are publishers of newsletters, magazines, websites, web portals, e-zines and the like exclusively devoted to senior citizens. It is a tough task to prepare a directory of such organizations but a small beginning has been made by Society for Serving Seniors, Secunderabad.

In the area of Elder Abuse a very large number of cases go unreported, as victims or their families are afraid of undue publicity. This is understandable but at the same time reporting of case studies anonymously (names changed and identity concealed) and further analysis by sociologists will only benefit the community. From this angle Senior Citizen Community should have immediate access to publishing / published resources relating to their problems. As already indicated networking of this section has no direct impact on EA except as noted here.

Website managers of portals dealing with Elder Care have already developed informal rapport and co-operation amongst is in full swing.

Errand Services, Listening Services: Senior citizens living alone require help in paying bills, buying medicines, shopping etc. Some Service Providers specialize in this area of running errands, keeping company, sending cooks for a temporarily for a day or so etc. Such hired hands need to be reliable and trustworthy. MayaCare in Pune, Hyderabad, Ahmadabad, Chennai, Mumbai, Bangalore, Delhi and Carewell Services in Hyderabad are offering such services, to name a few. Heritage Hospital in Hyderabad of course is a pioneer in this area but its services are limited to members who avail other services also. These are paid services for members.

Similarly lonely senior citizens crave to be listened. They have no one to talk to. The loneliness is miserable. SSS offers free listening service to elders over the phone. A group of 15 volunteers have signed up for giving this service. The 'customer' simply has to ring up the volunteer and he may go ahead talking. Here no counseling is done. No advice is offered. Simple plain ear-lending services are offered. For about a year Karmayog has been compiling details of such service providers all over India under "Lend your ears" section.

From the point of view of EA this is an excellent service area. Victims can pour their hearts. Many times simple listening helps. Networking amongst such agencies is essential. Volunteers may be swapped. As the service is rendered over telephone intercity networking is practicable.

Day Care Centers: Either as a part of Senior Citizens Associations or as independent units several Day Care Centers are available in cities. These are akin to Creche for children and toddlers. They engage the older people in indoor games, reading rooms, simple chatting and similar activities. Dignity, Harmony, Silver Innings, Nightingale and other NGOs offer these services at many places. In Hyderabad, Aasara, run by GHMC, has financed setting up of several (nearly 100) DCCs. They have compiled a directory too.

Informal chatting in DCC is a mitigative step in revelation and remedy of EA cases. Their networking is essential. Experience exchange will be invaluable.

Providers of Bedside Assistants and their training: Senior Citizens who are ill or bed ridden due to other reasons like fall/accidents etc require help in daily routines, taking medicines/injections etc. Family members may be busy or feel inadequate to take care of such elders. Bedside assistants, trained ayahs, semi qualified nurses (also known as caregivers) and others may be useful. A number of institutions offer short term and long term training for such healthcare professionals.

Heritage Hospital, Hyderabad; Sneha Deepam in Visakapatnam; Kherwadi Social Welfare Association, Mumbai; Carefit India Visakapatnam; Red Cross Society are some organizations offering training. NISD of MOSJE has been funding this activity for a long time and an online directory of some more than 700 trained persons is available on the web. (http://nice.nisd.gov.in/resource.php). The courses vary in duration, content, practical sessions etc.

Caregivers or BSAs by themselves are useful and available only in the city where they live. However networking of 1) Providers of such BSAs on hire 2) care giver trainers and training institutions, both within a state and across India will be useful. From EA point of view, we need to remember that, abuse by caregivers can not be ruled out, especially when the elder and BSA are left alone for long hours. Even sexual and physical abuse has been reported. Efficient networking would solve many problems, including EA.

Aged Care NGOs and VOs: A large number of NGOs and Voluntary Organizations in India claim to be working in the area of Aged Care. If we examine Planning Commission's "Partnership with NGO" program and its online directory, as a typical source for information, we find hundreds of NGOs registered over there. In AP alone, some 405 NGOs/VOs have something or the other to do with older persons though not all are exclusively dealing with aged care. (Aged care only - about thirty).

HelpAge (the largest with multicity operations), Silver Innings, Dignity Foundation, Harmony for Silvers, Nightingale Trust, COIN (Center for old in Need), Anurag, Agewell Foundation are some leading NGOs serving or caring for the aged and seniors.

Society for Serving Seniors is publishing a directory of NGOs/VOs dealing with aged care for Southern States. AP section is ready and others are under various stages of compilation.

Uniting all NGOs together both horizontally and hierarchically will be useful. Existence of so many NGO portals is proof of this need. In the case of EA, NGOS can play a major role: taking up cases to the tribunals, helping victims and abusers by arbitration, counseling family members at home, strengthening SCAs with volunteers etc are some solid ways of co-operation.

Part 3: Some Specific Organizations

In this part let us discuss a few Organizations that are important from networking point of view. These are in addition to those discussed earlier like AISCCON, ARDSI etc

Virtual Networks

There are two unique virtual networks for seniors in India

1. **Sss-global:** Society for Serving Seniors, Hyderabad has a web based Yahoo Group called sss-global. There about 600 senior citizens who are members. This is a virtual network of retirees exchanging info and experience via email only. All topics of interest and relevance to older people are discussed. This group was ranked 7th among some 1300 such groups by Yahoo some years ago. Daily exchange of messages is around thirty. This is a open (global) network for anyone above 55 and contents are readable by anyone, though for posting one has to be a member. (http://groups.yahoo.com/group/sss-global)
2. **Verdurez:** Verdurez is another virtual network exclusively for senior citizens. This is complete web portal offering all kinds of interaction among members. Newsletter, news collections, eBooks, stories, poems, articles, blogging facility, discussion groups, and personal mail exchange – in fact everything desirable is available. Only drawback I find is that it is a closed community as all exchanges occur within the members only. In fact very rich contributions made by members are not indexed by any search Engine like Google and are lost to outside

world. (http://www.verdurez.com). This essentially means that contributions do not get any publicity outside of Verdurian site which is detrimental to participants' interests.

In both the networks EA is an important subject and a lot of useful interaction takes place between victims and supporting friends.

Agewell Foundation, Delhi: The website talks about a huge network covering all states and UTs, 6500 volunteers, 540 districts reaching out to 4.8 million people. Though it is claimed that Aadhar helplines are active in 500plus districts I do not know of any activity in AP. The Aadhar program mentions almost everything connected with seniors' welfare - helplines, employment Exchange, school contacts, voluntary networks etc. If this can be revived and its resources put us, much of networking problems may be solved. Present activity appears to be confined to a few surveys and studies relating to ageing issues.

HelpAge: This is perhaps the largest active and alive organization ever since its establishment in 1978. All senior citizens associations, clubs, forums etc deal with middle class and upper class senior citizens who are otherwise comfortable financially. Only HelpAge (among larger NGOs) reaches down to Village level bringing elders together. It has HQ in Delhi, two national offices one each in Chennai and Kolkata and 55 branch offices in cities & towns. They play a major role in advocacy, direct help to poor seniors and fight for elders' rights.

INPEA: International Network for Prevention of Elder Abuse is a large global network exclusively taking care of Elders Rights and abuse. It has chapters in all major countries including India. Ms Mala Kapur Shankar Dass from Delhi takes care of Indian chapter. Established in 1997 in Massachusetts, USA, this organization provides guidance and help in observing World Elder Abuse Awareness Day on June 15th every year. Posters, literature and FAQ are provided. The

Local chapter collects information on activities in India for inclusion in a centralized report prepared by INPEA once a year. Apart from this events are organized in Delhi also. (http://www.inpea.net)

Summing up and recommendations: We have looked at various groups and types of organizations connected with senior citizens. Certain notable omissions in our discussion are: academic and research institutions connected with gerontology, geriatrics and geriatricians, government machinery (departments, commissariats, ministries etc) charged with this responsibility, philanthropic organizations with a slant towards senior citizens community etc. Institutions in the above areas here to be promoted to till the gap.

Keeping in view the groups that we have already discussed above, can we examine as to which organization(s) can or should take up the overall responsibility for uniting every body connected with elders? If the government establishes a separate National Council for older Persons with legal authority then that body can look into total networking needs. HelpAge is strong in rural areas but all other groups that we have seen above are out of their scope. It is only in recent years that HelpAge has its attention towards the urban seniors. AISCCON caters to SCAs only and that too for city based urban senior citizens. . If our requirements are narrow and we are concerned only with issues of EA and Neglect then INPEA (International Network for the Prevention of Elder Abuse) Chair for Asia and India could take up the lead and responsibility of creating a network from EA point of view.

"National Alliance of Senior Citizens associations in India" – NASCAI – that came up a couple of years ago could perhaps serve this purpose. Some sort of voluntary coming together is already taking place as a part of organizing Senior Citizens National Protest Day (Appendix 1). This is the best opportunity to forge unity among all disparate entities /

groups. This is essential to achieve results in advocacy issues as well. Senior Citizens must rise as a single voice.

In my view total and comprehensive networking of ALL organizations connected the elderly should be attempted. It is high time we do this - after all, the target of everyone concerned is the older persons –they should benefit ultimately. Networking is the only way.

APPENDIX 1

Some Prominent Organizations in the area of Aged care in India who are recently networking for a common cause of protesting against Governmental indifference

(Notice how this is a mixture of SCAs, NGOs, Pensioners Groups, VOs etc)

1. All India Senior Citizens' Confederation [AISCCON]
2. National Alliance of Senior Citizens Associations of India [NASCAI]
3. Bharat Pensioners' Samaj (BPS)
4. RREWAS – retired Railway Employees Association, Rewa, MP
5. Respect Age International (RAI)
6. Indian Federation of Ageing (InFA)
7. Indian Association of Retired Persons [IARP]
8. Andhra Pradesh Senior Citizens' Confederation
9. Federation of Senior Citizens' of Maharashtra [FESCOM]
10. Federation of Senior Citizens of UP [FESCUP]
11. Federaion of AP Senior Citzens' Organisations [FAPSCO]
12. Kerala Federation of Senior Citizens' Associations
13. Karnatak Senior Citizens Federation
14. Tamil Nadu Senior Citizens' Confederation

15. Silver Innings Foundation [Mumbai]
16. Delhi Federation of Senior Citizens' Associations
17. Gujarat Federation of Senior Citizens
18. Prantiya Varishtha Nagrik Mahasangh [MP]
19. Varishtha Nagrik Sansthan [Rajasthan]
20. Senior Citizens Council of Assam
21. All India Bank Retirees Federation
22. Nightingales Medical Trust
23. Kerala Sr.Citizens' Forum
24. HelpAge India
25. Dignity Foundation
26. Harmony Silver Foundation
27. Anugruha

APPENDIX 2

List of Abbreviations used in this Paper

(Acronyms of institutions already covered in Appendix 1 are not repeated here)

Abbreviation	Expansion
1	2
AASARA	Helpline set up by GHMC and run by HelpAge, Hyderabad
AED	Assistive and Enabling Devices
BSA	Bedside assistant (aka: caregiver, ayah)
COIN	Center for Old in Need
DCC	Day Care Center
EA	Elder Abuse (and Neglect)
FAQ	Frequently Asked Questions
GHMC	Greater Hyderabad Municipal Corporation
MOHFW	Ministry of Health and Family Welfare

1	2
MOSJE	Ministry of Social Justice and Empowerment
MWPSCA	Maintenance and Welfare of Parents and Senior Citizens Act 2007
NISD	National Institute of Social Defense (part of MOSJE)
OAH	Old Age Home
SC	Senior Citizen
SCA	Senior Citizens Association
SSS	Society for Serving Seniors

Networking of NGOs for Ageing and Human Rights

— Sailesh Mishra

Ageing is a natural process, which inevitably occurs in human life cycle. It brings with a host of challenges in the life of the elderly, which are mostly engineered by the changes in their body, mind, thought process and the living patterns. Population ageing is a global phenomenon having implications on all aspects of human life in every society.

In India Aged (above 60 yrs) as per 2001 Census are 7.5% of total population i.e. 76 million. The Estimated Elderly Population in 2009 @ average 8% is 90 million. According to UN by 2050, nearly 20% of India's population will comprise of people over the age of 60 years.

Everyone in this world faces varieties of problems. But there is indescribable suffering in old age. No one wants to grow old. But the force of inevitable time everyone is forced to grow old. An aged person now termed, as *Senior Citizen* becomes unwanted property in the family. This is the harsh reality. Therefore, it becomes necessary to make you aware your rights.

Human Rights are universal, civil, political, economic, social and cultural rights and belong to all human beings, including older people. Human Rights of aged are explicitly set out in the Universal Declaration and International Covenants as well as in the Constitution of India.

The U.N. General Assembly on December 16, 1991 adopted 18 principles which are organized into 5 clusters:

- Independence
- Participation
- Care
- Self-fulfilment
- Dignity of the older persons

When people cannot articulate their needs and fight for their rights they need an advocate to play that role for them, to make sure that their voices can be heard. Societies are judged by the care, respect and well-being of those people and groups of people who are disadvantaged, such as the disabled or profoundly ill. Older people cannot always shout loudly enough or for long enough to make the changes that are required to give them the proper care, happiness, and dignity they deserve.

The purpose of the Networking & Advocacy is to assist and support older people to articulate, exercise and defend their rights and to fully participate in both the minor and major decisions affecting their lives

The New York NGO Committee on Ageing works collaboratively to promote and support a United Nations (UN) Convention for the Rights of Older Persons. Its mention in NPOP 1999 that "The State alone cannot provide all the services needed by older persons". Private sector agencies cater to a rather small paying segment of the population. The National Policy recognizes the NGO sector as a very important institutional mechanism to provide user friendly affordable services to complement the endeavours of the State in this direction.

Voluntary effort will be promoted and supported in a big way and efforts made to remedy the current uneven spread both within a state and between states. There will be continuous dialogue and communication with NGOs on ageing issues and on services to be provided. Networking, exchange of information and interactions among NGOs will be facilitated.

Networking brings with it innovative approaches of working. The true creativity of an NGO lies in creating networks of information, innovation and interaction that enables people to communicate, to share and to receive, effecting positive social change in the long run. Bring people together locally and globally, and focus attention on key issues for discussion, deliberation and consensus is true networking. A united Front will help to promote rights of older persons by engaging as many NGOs national/ global and to develop a network of information sharing (positive and negative), evidence of age discrimination as well as good practices of advocacy tools used to positively influence national governments in support of the rights of older persons.

In order to protect the rights of older persons and move the agenda on ageing forward, the efforts of all stakeholders must be combined and coordinated so that a **society for all ages** can become a reality.

Together we CAN & we WILL give New Dimension to Ageing in India.

Index